House *of* Sparrows

ALSO BY
BETSY SHOLL

Otherwise Unseeable
Rough Cradle
Late Psalm
Coastal Bop
Don't Explain
The Red Line
Pick a Card
Rooms Overhead
Appalachian Winter
Changing Faces

House of *Sparrows*

NEW AND SELECTED POEMS

Betsy Sholl

The University of Wisconsin Press

THE UNIVERSITY OF WISCONSIN PRESS

1930 Monroe Street, 3rd Floor
Madison, Wisconsin 53711-2059
uwpress.wisc.edu

Gray's Inn House, 127 Clerkenwell Road
London EC1R 5DB, United Kingdom
eurospanbookstore.com

Printed in the United States of America

This book may be available in a digital edition.

Library of Congress Cataloging-in-Publication Data
Names: Sholl, Betsy, author.
Title: House of sparrows : new and selected poems / Betsy Sholl.
Other titles: Wisconsin poetry series.
Description: Madison, Wisconsin : The University of Wisconsin Press, [2019] |
            Series: Wisconsin poetry series
Identifiers: LCCN 2018040967 | ISBN 9780299323042 (pbk. ; alk. paper)
Subjects: | LCGFT: Poetry.
Classification: LCC PS3569.H574 H68 2019 | DDC 811/.54—dc23
LC record available at https://lccn.loc.gov/2018040967

For Isabella, Max,
Wyatt, and Rhyse

And the emptiness turns its face to us
and whispers
"I'm not empty, I am open"

—TOMAS TRANSTRÖMER

Contents

From **THE RED LINE** (1992)

From **DON'T EXPLAIN** (1997)

From **LATE PSALM** (2004)

From **ROUGH CRADLE** (2009)

Acknowledgments

Heartfelt thanks to the editors of the following magazines where these poems first appeared:

Brilliant Corners: "Walking Paradise Blues," *"Trouble in Mind,"* "Elegy and Blues";

Field: "Imago Dei," "To a Bat Fallen in the Street," "Philomela";

Image: "Making Dinner I Think about Poverty," "Daybreak, Winter," "House of Sparrows," "Knock";

Plume: "Capital I," "In the Aftermath";

Negative Capability: "Starry Night";

New Ohio Review: "'We Buy, Sell, Trade'";

Numero Cinq: "Apple," *"Fortune"*;

Salamander: "Her Story";

Solstice: "Night Class in Wind," "The Undoing";

Sojourners: "Petition";

Upstreet: "One Night the Wind Got Wild, Then Wilder, And," "Concerning the Soul."

Special thanks to the editors and publishers of the original books: the University of Pittsburgh Press, Alice James Books, the University of Wisconsin Press; and to the many friends who read this manuscript in process: Suzan Aizenberg, Linda Aldrich, Ted Deppe, Nancy Eimers, Sascha Feinstein, Lee Hope, Dave Jauss, Leslie Ullman, Estha Weiner, all my colleagues at Vermont College of Fine Arts, and the Portland poetry group; special thanks to Ron Wallace for longtime support; and to Doug Sholl: even through the fog you are light.

House of Sparrows

NEW POEMS

APPLE

Crisp air, press of ladder rung on instep,
        tree sway and dappled light, then stem twist
                and the weight of apple in hand—

reaching through that leafy green, did we ask
        what else we were after? Some desire
                to possess the whole splendid day, sunglint

on grass, September's slow withdrawal,
        the drying leaves sparse now, so the apples
                were little flames. Strange that we make

one fruit both medicine and poison,
        prescribed and forbidden, as if everything's
                mixed, and there's no forgetting that darker

hunger at work, blind to the damage it does,
        ego's bad apple, poison in the star
                and gravity, gravity, gravity.

But also windfalls in wet grass—paradox
        of fortune—how sweet for the bees and wasps
                who find the cores warmed by the sun

into a heady liquor, and sip. Once
        we had a wooden apple made with such skill
                more than one person picked it up

thinking to bite, until our dog finally did.
        We found it under the couch, splintered
                and pocked, and with stern voices banished him

to the yard—as if once down the stairs
        he wouldn't happily enter that bright world
                of rock and dirt, nuthatch, beetle, squirrel.

ONE NIGHT THE WIND GOT WILD, THEN WILDER, AND

what were we thinking? A school night,
our whole yard getting tossed, as if the wind had a warrant.

But something to see: the full moon sailing through clouds,
the biggest wind we'd ever known.

Young as you were, you'd been through fire and flood,
then this cornfield and our new tin house,

a fairy-tale world of cows and bluebirds, unlocked doors,
wide fields surrounded by hills.

So we crooned, *Wake up*, to your sleep-soft face—
Do you remember?

That wind we could spread our arms and practically ride.
We didn't want you to think: wolf licking its lips,

puffing at the roof tiles, the world howling down the chimney,
saying what fodder we were.

You stood in the doorway rubbing your eyes as old rags flapped up
and the plastic on the woodpile ripped free.

Slowly you grinned and began to twirl with us
in the moonstruck stubble.

Our nightclothes belled in the wind. Fistfuls, armfuls—
what straw to hurl.

My sleepy darling, we wanted to give you a different tale,
milkweed wands and a world happy to huff itself up.

———

4

As close as we'll ever get to flight—
those lawn chairs clattering down the road, the cow gate groaning,

and the straps that held our trailer down
twanging like an eerie guitar.

HER STORY

Johnson City, Tennessee

What a ruckus—those fricatives inside
that truck, spitting out roadside grit
digging itself in deeper.

Overhead the sky's one eye looks down.
Near full it rose, rusty as the truck's
undersides and dented with shadows.

Below, out of gas, trapped, that truck
hardly looks like it once jumped red lights,
gunned through town, took hairpins

with a squeal. As to the woman inside
pounding the wheel, she just saw her man
of fourteen years take off with somebody

blond and younger. She's got a fifth
on the seat beside her, a pistol,
a box of ammo already emptied out

into every Slow Curve, Falling Rock,
Soft Shoulder she passed downshifting
on the upgrade. *Who you think does that?*

she'll ask months later, then grin.
But now, inside that bucket of rust,
it's just her hollowed out, a full bottle

of sleep, and the moon overhead
watching, so she points her pistol,
pulls the trigger and laughs, bitter

as the pills she unscrews and scatters
like buckshot across the road.
Then she leans back into liquor's drift.

Come morning, an old man will drive up,
peer in, see all that trouble
and hook up chains to haul her out.

He'll give her gas enough to get to town,
tell her, *Now you never mind, Honey,
you just go on*—and she will. She will.

STARRY NIGHT

Once I had several dreams in the same week, each telling me
I could let the worst happen and step away, alive in a field so bright
no way to paint it but with thick globs and swirls of green. So,

let others build their barricades against disappointment and death,
against what ruin will or will not strike with its one blue bolt to the heart,
its crows crowding in, stifling the sky, iron everywhere.

Let the goldfinches disappear into this pair of young maples, deep into
the leaves. When they fall, come autumn, we'll find two thimble-sized nests,
thistle down and milkweed tied to a crook with spider thread.

Who needs straight lines? All those theories about how Van Gogh
got to his whirling stars—absinthe, cataracts, madness.
But can't someone let the facts go and just paint how it feels

under a star-splattered sky, light splotched, night kissed, and for once
no longer locked out? A moment irony would never allow,
and bitterness would surely miss with its grim resentment

that counts every slight. But how my grandfather's garden flourished!
Grandfather of shame, of the straight raised cane, harsh word, stony
silence the earth kept trying to woo. From the roof of his chicken coop

my sisters and I watched the last finches twitter and dip
toward their roosts, as the cedar's lace grew dark, and the night sky
got ready to bloom. Beneath us, grapes nestled in their leaves,

pumpkins grew fat as hassocks, and potatoes slowly
inched out their eye beams like stars hidden in the dirt—
or what could have been stars if allowed to shine.

FORTUNE

Dante says she's a kind of heavenly worker,
not quite an angel but more than a force
as she turns the wheel from famine to feast,
making failure last no longer than fame.
But failure, that big red F at the top of the page,

stops me in my tracks. Once I thought I could
just take it, not write the paper on Freud
and Buber. But the thought so frightened me,
my whole body felt an electric fizz.
"F— that," I must have muttered, then sat down

to write, living on muffins and coffee
a whole week, dropping a small fortune
in the payphone, crying to my boyfriend
about Freud's money metaphor, his belief that
women spend all our psychic energy

just growing up. . . . So that little *f* checked
on our birth certificate freezes the wheel?
Our fate's rigged, and any faith we have
is just infantile delusion, oceanic feeling
with no base in reality or reason?

Tap water coffee and Buber all night—
how I hoped for some splendid refutation.
Against reason he tells stories: Here is
Rabbi Isaak pacing a bridge in Krakow
because he's dreamed a treasure hidden there.

Here's the guard stopping him, then scoffing, "Ha!
If I believed in dreams I'd have to go
to the house of a Jew named Isaak and dig
under his stove." So, the rabbi hurries home
and finds that treasure, as if faith—or fate—

is all detour and surprise, stepping out
to find the way back in. With his fortune,
the rabbi builds a house of prayer—because,
Herr Doktor, what to do with such a gift
but pour it out into more giving?

MAKING DINNER I THINK
ABOUT POVERTY—

I mean the kind saints praise and scripture
calls blessed, the kind that inherits heaven
where maybe what's left of us will be

more like a clear broth than the vegetables
and meat we chop up here, as the radio
blasts war, soup kitchen fills,

and down the block a crowd gathers
around two men yelling their different stories
to the cop as an ambulance wails off.

In its wake, I go back to cutting carrots
and beets, gazing into their concentric rings.
Everything with its secret heart,

Saint Francis says, where it's better to be
prey than predator, better to step into
the net than be the one who rigs it.

Poverty, he says, a word so pure
it can't be hyped. It sees into the dark
vessels of the heart, where the blessed know

what they lose, what sinks to the bottom,
enriches the stock—which we will ladle out
to those shuffling in with their empty bowls,

as if they follow the saint's hard recipe,
the one that says: Put everything in the pot
and let fire take over.

WALKING PARADISE BLUES

"Bitter, another man's salty bread, lord, lord,
bitter the climb up somebody else's stairs"—
Dante sings a kind of terza rima blues.

In our time it could be Jimmy Rogers's
"Walkin' by myself, hope you'll understand"
backed up on harp by Big Walter Horton

who played Chicago streets on warehouse break
for tips from lunchtime execs come slumming.
No harmonica cupped to the mic for Dante,

no train whistle wail, battered guitar whine.
Still, he got down, got low down, talking back
to the city's shut gate. Knew how the spit

you have to tap out, tipping the harp,
first you have to pour in.

White as she was and more English than that,
my grandma knew the blues. What spit I got
I got from her wet kisses. Got the blues

from how she asked her brother, big time doc,
said, "My pockets are empty. Can you lend a hand?"
And he with the six servants, Cadillac wife,

sent her a twenty. Cash, no note. Bitter
the spit she swallowed back saying thanks.
Bitter the bills unpaid, flickering lights.

But sweet those gut-bucket blues Big Walter
wailed, and she hummed along as she trudged,
stuck self and hell-sludge to light, oh yeah.

Sweet those jelly arms, lips happy to smooch.
Never had to knock twice on Grandma's door.

Good welcome was Dante's paradise too,
walking those dark blues into starry light.
"Play the street when the record deal don't come,"

Big Walter must've told himself. For Grandma
it was, "Give all you got." And she gave more
even to birds than her brother ever had.

I'm witness to the wispy hair she pulled
from her brush, then leaned out the window
for those high flyers to swoop in and snatch.

Soul, I'm talking about, what Big Walter
blew through bent notes, lonely so you know
somebody's been down that road before.

Lord, they sang. Wore out how many shoes—
one eye fixed on the grit, one on the stars.

TO A BAT FALLEN IN THE STREET

Crumpled carbon paper, I thought.
Then you moved, humped yourself up
and collapsed, using your wings
like crutches, straining to inch off
the street onto somebody's lawn,
as if you knew the difference.

I bent close enough to see:
your small cat ears, gargoyle shape.
But couldn't bring myself to touch,
to help, as if I were what you were
made to scare off. Terrible,
your struggle to cross. I cringed,
wanting a door to shut, wanting to jog off

like easy belief, thinking the stars
are pure light, not firestorms raging.
But there you were, a glimpse of God
nobody wants—broken body, dark night
with shattered doors, and what sonar
beyond my ears still singing?

"WE BUY, SELL, TRADE"

Ideas are one thing and what happens is another.
—JOHN CAGE

Weather or axe—who neglected or hacked
to make this bag of piano keys, this

clatter of loose scales in a paper sack,
fifty-two whites, the yellow of stained teeth,

a few of them chipped: some upright or grand,
its music collapsed in a racket of chainsaws

cutting up belly and legs for scrap.
Warped wood, thunk of stuck notes—

what undid that instrument, till it became
a jalopy of sound put up on blocks,

eye sore, ear sore, cat perch, wooden elephant
in a drafty room, its strings turned to rust,

felts crumbled, until under its lid
Mozart was mute, Bach battered and gagged,

Handel held captive?
Nothing to do but burn that jail down,

all the way to this set of keys
minus instrument, keys minus door,

minus locket or house, left in a dusty shop.
It hurts to think that before these keys

were pulled out like teeth, they were teeth,
to think of those marvelous creatures

with big leafy ears who swayed in grasslands
far from our drawing rooms—how hunters

must have heard the pitiful cry when one fell,
and still they sawed off its tusks.

Now the instrument its dying made
has been undone, reduced to a junk shop find

for someone to turn into earrings or pins,
or just carry around like the eye tooth,

knucklebone of a saint, asking,
What isn't made from another's breaking?

PHILOMELA

Dear nightingale hiding in green thickets,
I don't want to think of the girl

who couldn't tell her story, how nothing she sang
said what happened to her, her voice smudged

like wet ink the left hand blurs as it writes.
Well, worse than that—the knife at her throat,

the whole dark alley of him, errant star
burning inside her, then burning her out,

the red of her, the words. Her tale
like no tapestry you'd hang on the wall.

But the sweetness of your song, Bird,
it tears at the heart, as if hidden deep

in every family there's a story like this.
So in ours.

There was a man who couldn't sleep nights
hearing your song outside his window.

Long before his daughters ever told,
he tore himself into an endless tremor.

He'd sputter and cough, choke on his food
and seem to deserve the more pity for that.

What is a story but a nest, and what is a nest
but a vessel made for breakage and flight?

Those girls were not made for the story
they had to tell. But tell it they did.

Out of such troubled bodies, a shattered song,
out of the thicket, pouring forth.

TROUBLE IN MIND

Since the twenties, the song's been passing
through singer after singer, Lightnin' Hopkins,
Nina Simone, and, released after his death,

the voice of Johnny Cash: "Trouble in mind,
I'm blue, but I won't be blue always."
That's the hope of the invalids, the blind

and lame lying beside the temple pool,
waiting, the Gospel says, for the angel
to come down and trouble the water.

Then the first one in gets healed. But only
one each time and nobody knows when.
Trouble (v): "to disturb, mix,

make cloudy, confuse, bewilder." So,
the angel comes to stir things up. Disrupt.
And out of what blue does that angel come,

air or despair? What of roadside bombs,
whole cities leveled, old and new Jim Crow,
minds broken beyond repair? Even angels

must tremble at troubles so deep,
or at the thought: one skid, a cyclist is gone.
And what if you or I were the driver

sending him over the guardrail, down the ravine?
What if we're citizens of a country built on
the anguish of others? (What country?

Every country.) A "cup of trembling,"
the prophet says, "a cup of staggering"
to those who prosper on the backs of the poor.

Jesus says, "Let the day's trouble be
sufficient for the day," as if the promise
never was clear sailing, but instead

———

the angel's wing, the riled water.
As if trouble sometimes is the bridge
the wind kicks up, the waves rising over

the gunwales. Jesus sleeps in the stern,
as the disciples cry out, "Don't you care
we're perishing?"—men who, without the storm,

the swamped boat, might have sailed easily on,
not thinking how deep trouble can be,
how frail the vessel, the many lost at sea,

on land, in cities crushed. And so the angel,
that great wind or wing, stirs the waters, stirs
the soul, troubles the mind of the singer

into song, that pool anyone can enter,
voice after voice, hoping it might be true:
"I'm blue, but I won't be blue always. . . ."

HOUSE OF SPARROWS

What if every time we saw the word *sorrow*
we switched it to *sparrow*?

> *For my life is spent with sparrows . . .*
> *With drunkenness and sparrows . . .*

Or if it went the other way, the song would be,
> *His eye is on the sorrow. . . .*

My eye's on the neighbor's eaves,
and the copper-roofed house we put up in our yard,

its many rooms, multiple nests, generations—
as if we brought this clamor on ourselves,

this hurdy-gurdy, rabble, host and quarrel
of sparrows
          mixed with the morning radio

broadcasting a bombed hospital, bodies
under fallen roof tiles, shards of over-voice and wailing,

while outside birds flare up, knock each other off the feeder,
sparrows the color of rubble, of dust and mud,

burnt cars, blown-out windows, of wreckage
they could roost in, the earth a house of sparrows

on Sparrow Street, hunger house, and woe
to the poor who are spared nothing,

who gather at borders to beg and forage, are sold
      two for a penny, five for two cents.

And yet doesn't it say the Lord God
attends—bends down to count

each one shot, starved, buried in rubble?—
A man of sparrows and acquainted with grief,

who says, when I bow my head,
      Sparrows are better than laughter.

And to the rabble, the wailing, the how, the when,
who says,
      Your sparrows will turn to joy—

KNOCK

I wouldn't call gulping a glass of ale
and backhanding foam off your upper lip
a form of devotion, or the refusal
to laugh at an off-color joke a sign
of reverence. But I can imagine God,

a wounded rat in one hand, a soothing song—
I do not say on his lips. No, it's snowmelt
running along the street toward the sewer,
and in the gutter, huge and dead, is the rat—
all of which, why not, might as well be God,

as different from what we suppose as fire
from firefly, ash from snow falling
on your shoulder. And just try to push
a baby carriage past a dead rat without
a shudder and that sudden "ew"—the sound

a young woman with all her life ahead
makes at foreign and cringe-worthy death,
the opposite of breasts fat with milk.
Years ago, and still that rat's gnawing
through my brain like something God might do

with his *first shall be last* and *fear not,
little flock: sell all you have.* That rat,
the size of a cat, so maybe I could have
imagined it purring, not chewing its way
into the crib at night. Fat chance.

To love a rat, a mosquito, junkie,
an ex-con, Exxon, the tough girl who shoves you
against your locker, the kid with razor scars
on his cheekbones looking sullen as if
you're a pigeon to be x'ed off the street—

it doesn't even sound easy. They say
the church down the block has a bone shard
chipped from the jaw of someone who laid hands
on a fevered girl and she sprang up cured.
Size of a fingernail, kept in a box.

The church is a box they open a little,
but not too much. So God has to seep in,
as on that unnaturally warm New Year's day
full of car exhaust, trolley clatter, shy men
outside the bodega who've watched for months

and finally get to coo at my new baby: God
has to move through snowmelt, uncollected trash,
burn smells from the torched warehouse; has to
stand there and knock at the church door.
Wet fur, twitchy whiskers.

CONCERNING THE SOUL

Someone must have been rushing home from a party
or football rally, and maybe she was high, so hardly noticed
when our tree snatched her bouquet of yellow balloons.

Or maybe she did and tried to jump, grab them back,
like that story of the little fox leaping to get at grapes
dangling just out of reach, then *forget it!*—she trots off.

But oh, the afterlife. How it teases and haunts,
how it bleeds into this life.

No good tossing a stick to bring down balloons
if you want them unbroken.

And you can't throw a bottle at them either
without leaving its sharp glitter on the street.

Thus we woke next morning to a mess of leftover effervescence,
a dozen suns shining through salty fog.

For weeks they clustered and hung, as slowly one,
then another shriveled, each in turn dwindled,
grown flaccid, puckered like raisins.

Then one day they were gone, wind-blasted,
blizzard-blown gone, leaving only what we hadn't noticed,
a slim white ribbon dangling like a strand of DNA,

a streamer from that vanished celebration—
not the bright yellow bluster of the thing itself, but a string,
tiny icon pointing to—

what once was, or to how far it has gone?

Such thoughts all winter, then summer, now winter again,
and the string's still here, sperming, worming in wind,
firmly tied at one end, loose at the other,

unraveling thread from snow's hem,
rippling out, slackening—

———

THE UNDOING

Sidewalk bricks unmortared by winter's freeze and thaw—
    no looking up here, we take mincing steps,
and our talk turns to everything undone—frayed
    bootlaces, laundry, taxes, bills, books—so many
books piled up unread, sliding off the nightstand.
    Even the universe, you say, is not done
expanding into whatever lies beyond. Once I thought
    aging meant arriving at a plateau beyond struggle
and change, a thought first challenged by church ladies
    in Big Stone Gap, Virginia, sitting with Mrs. J
in the hospital when I went calling, surprised that
    with all her faith she panicked at an inch of river
running through her cellar. Didn't belief mean
    she was beyond such undoing? Oh how those ladies
threw back their heads and laughed! Slapped their thighs,
    Who-eee, then laughed again, *Oh honey!*
Now, along these winter streets, ice hangs in thick cords
    where gutters have been overrun. You grab me
as I start to slip, and it brings back that Cambridge night
    we held each other on sidewalks full of glare ice
and packed snow, when behind us a window flew open,
    and an old woman's frail voice called, *Yoo-hoo,*
as she waved a change purse and asked us to buy
    groceries for her at the corner store. How is it
I can recall the small shriek of that raised window,
    and yet have no memory of taking the purse,
returning with milk, bread, eggs jiggling in their little cups?
    Could we have left her unanswered, dangling there?
No memory of the restaurant where we were headed,
    or what came after, either. It's all undone.
As if the night stopped there, on that street,
    midsentence, whatever we'd been saying.
The night, quick jolt of window thrown open,
    paper-thin hand reaching out.

IN THE AFTERMATH

It's all shovel and dig, snow banks
done up to glow, getting dirty.

All shove and dog, the world half riddle,
half proof. It's fiddle and roof,

the *deedle dum* and shrug of prayer.
Icy streets, mincing steps, and later—

why not dance, sore shins into whirlwind,
till we can't tell ourselves from God?

Of course we all know: Afterlife =
empty wallets, no shoes in the coffin.

And we know, before walking on ice,
to pull our hands out of our pockets.

Meanwhile somebody's taking the long view,
reminding us mountains turn to silt.

Or sometimes I think *silk*—those Japanese screens
on which tiny people cross a bridge

overlooking a steep gorge,
as if that's what we were wanting before

we forgot: to be happily effaced by awe,
that moment talk defers to silence.

Oh imperfect tense, oh past, unfinished
and progressive, help me

to actually be doing this,
stepping onto that tenuous bridge

beside the water's plummet.

NIGHT CLASS IN WIND

Will God, or somebody else, give me the power to
breathe into my canvases . . . the sigh of prayer and
of sadness, . . . of rebirth?
—MARC CHAGALL

Outside, louder than street noise, the wind
is making itself heard. Trees, wires, loose casements—

the whole world's its instrument. What does it want?—
banging at these windows like desperation's ghost,

rattling the students bent over their words, letters
on the page that look like something the wind could snatch,

like feathers or leaves, or an eddy of roadside cinders
swirling up and strewn against the glass, scattered

thought, storm-tossed marks impossible to read,
like the lines my friend watched a concierge scribble

in a foreign city, as he grew sicker, delirious,
was put in a cab, the note pinned to his jacket: address

of the only doctor in town who spoke his language,
or instructions to whom it may concern: how to give

his soul to the wind. . . . Here, this wind snatches
other notes from the practice room next door

before the fiddler can gather them into a tune,
as if it howled at the thought those notes were his.

And the fiddle? You can't say it weeps,
though something in the sound grieves, perhaps for the tree

it was made from, or maybe it's the horsetail strands
pulled taut in the bow that still half know

they were once nearly liquid, flowing through fields.
Fevered and alone, my friend says he let fear go

as he floated across the city like something out of Chagall's
klezmer soul—that fiddler drifting over rooftops,

playing sob into dance. Goat foot, dove eye,
horse tossing its head, music and leaves aswirl, the wind

doing what wind does—blowing through shirttails,
through fever and thought, as if its job were to loosen, to lift

every blessed thing, even our words in this room,
played like laundry on a line—

union suit, housecoat, knickers—our pens
holding them down, our pens letting them go.

ELEGY AND BLUES

Morning in your brother's place after he's gone
the alarm startles us with a gravel croon:

You gotta get up, if you wanna get down.
Gritty voice of an old blues man,

or rain-smudged page torn from the grieving soul
of Cesar Vallejo: *Well, don't we rise, really,*

in order to go down? Around us, saxophones
not yet starting to mold in their cases—

tenor, alto, bari—and that voice again
after the snooze, bending *up* and *down* like notes,

as if *down's* not just a good time in some club,
but more like the dark oven of Vallejo's heart

grieving for the poor. And poor must be how
your brother felt when the doctors sent him home,

nothing more to do, breath drained, strength gone.
His last gigs he sat to play where once he swung

those horns side to side, leaned back to wail that sax
straight to the marrow. Now grief makes your memory

reverse the clock's tune, so you hear the flip side:
You gotta get down, if you wanna get up—

Gospel of the blues, and equally true,
come through rough-hewn prophets, raw voices

recorded in the field on primitive machines,
so the singer's breath and cleared throat

seep inside to wake us at night, whispering,
We got all the shades, sky to bruise, ocean

to eye, and we're singing to you. It's a tune
hard to refuse, this getting down,

as if rising's just a ruse, somebody else
paying our dues. And how those gut-bucket blues

your brother played tugged on us all. Club
after club, who didn't look down those lonely

railroad irons, willing to be no one, anyone,
feeling our own train-gone, motherless-child,

midnight hues, under that moon of light-struck
brass, now sealed in a velvet dark?

Last time we heard him play we left the club,
our bodies all echo and reverb. Looking up

under city lights we hoped for stars,
though hadn't the music already told us

it would take a darker night, a darker night,
my love, for them to show?

CAPITAL *I*

Beyond *ibis, ice axe, igloo, ingot,*
whole pages in the dictionary's I section
have no pictures. After all, how do you
illustrate *impact, impart, inchoate?*

But nine countries start with I, which you can list
in the middle of the night when insomnia strikes
if you're like so many of us now, asking
ourselves in those late-night interrogations

how well we have spent our lives. Impaled
by the swinging light bulb's harsh shadow,
who can't accuse themselves of too little
or much: ambition, greed, kindness, love?

One friend asks if he made a terrible mistake
leaving music for an academic life. Another
now sees that she never fully gave herself to art.
A third looks at his own impatience

and wonders who the hell he thought he was.
"We all live in a capital I," I sang
along with my kids watching *Sesame Street,*
as if instilling that sturdy castle of self,

not thinking someday I'd want to take off
those imperial robes and walk incognito
through market stalls, toasting locals at the inn:
Here's to age making paupers of us all!

Even in Whitman's great *Song of Myself,*
the first word may be "I," but the last is "you,"
as if that's our ultimate itinerary.
Once in Ireland, in Doolin, when the seas

were too wild for the ferry run to Inisheer,
my love and I stood on shore as waves rose
to magnificent peaks, then thundered down
into a white scatter and seethe of foam. Wind

gathered us up in its roar and swirl, until
there was nothing more to want, but that
moment on those rocks, at the bright edge
of everything beyond, utterly immersed.

IMAGO DEI

Nail parings, tooth bits, rubbed eyelashes, blood—
what if over the broken bedstead of the past

there hovers for each of us an effigy
made from all the parts we let go,

the shot sparrows of ourselves, lost pages,
beetle-eaten leaves? Some nights

the world is a banging shutter
or a dream of crows scraping the sky,

some nights a tape measure coiled
and sleeping in a drawer.

What if along the road, in a truck's tailwind
you found a black stone with a white

quartz cross embedded within?
Surely, it would be a sin to want back

all the skin we've shed,
holding on when all instructions say, *Let go*—

of these shards, these shadowy parts,
scars and wounds,

till they're gathered up
into a kind of angel-other,

all particle and wave, moving
like metal shavings toward

some great magnet whose force
is invisible until it inhabits us.

DAYBREAK, WINTER

Now light fills the tree outside our window—
tree whose fruit, when it comes, only the birds,
and just a few of them, want to eat, tree

that turns stiff and dry midsummer, rushing
the season, so we fear the city will come
and butcher it, though so far it's been spared

because in spring it still swarms with thousands
of petals, white as moths done with hunger,
white as tiny brides flittering in the breeze,

asking "Will I be happy? Is this a mistake?"—
or the question too few of us ever ask, "Will I
make him (or her) happy? Will I be able to love

when it's hard?" Hard like waking for sunrise
midsummer—or reading Saint John of the Cross
who says light first comes to us as darkness.

In my dream it could have been the saint's voice
that broke through some penthouse party, asking
"Do you want to stay here in your red dress,

with your expensive wine and smart chatter,
or do you want something more?" And how
was my dream-self tapping at walls to know

one would creak open onto a dark corridor
where "more" became a slow procession, pilgrims
in hooded robes turning from everything bright?

At least our tree gleams—*ours* because it's grown
higher than the upstairs windows, so we half dream
we live in its branches, ours because we tell

_____

the seasons by it, blossom and leaf-fall-too-soon
and winter's bare limbs, stripped like a saint's
uplifted arms taking whatever comes as love.

Once I fell out of a tree. Watching, my love
thought it was my death he saw. Maybe it was—
that bright thicket of leaves I crashed through

like a clumsy bird, or like a girl left back
and too big for her grade. I felt that slow,
suspended in twig-snap and fluttering green,

not grasping it was big trouble. I still don't
know how I got to where people stood over me,
asking, "Can you move this? Do you feel that?"

Whole minutes are blacked out. A young man said,
"If she walks away from this, I'll believe in God."
I don't know if he did. But I got up, stepped

across the gap of lost time and torn boughs
into the sweet weight of sunlight striking earth
every second, whether we notice or not.

Dawn in winter. Delicate, as if a painter
had licked the tip of the brush for fine work—
first twig, then trunk, the light made visible

by what it touches. Years, and still that dream
haunts me, its deep voice, dark corridor
with torches flaring, guttering on damp walls,

and those hooded figures, all foot-scrape
and drone, that slow hypnotic hum.
It went on and on, forever I thought,

until in the distance a low door appeared.
Through it a light-bathed garden and a tree
that may have been ordinary, hard to say

after all that darkness, after the dream
bent me so I could pass into—how easy
it sounds—the brightness, the green.

PETITION

You who sees through our windows like light,
sees the thoughts we hide in the oven of ourselves,

and the staircase on which we freeze between *yes* and *no*,
you who knows the betrayal inside every word,

speak to me in sleep what waking I cannot hear.
Show me the flames, the house falling of its own weight,

the terrible boxcars, and if there are still jewels
in the world, let there be so many

there's no need to pocket a single one. . . .
When the world shrinks to a leaf underfoot,

to a beggar's soiled trousers
and the punk who kicks him awake,

when love's drudgery grows blind to its own miracle,
you who hides in thick leaves that will fall

and mulch the earth, who speaks in bird shadow,
cloud script, the toothless spit of the old—

open the storehouse of wonder,
mix the palette of sleep, till on waking

the world, even in darkness, is so present
there is nothing to hide, withhold, or hoard.

Let the banging shutter sing,
and the storm-riven tree shake its tangled locks.

Invisible host, ghostwriter, spirit grocer,
it isn't for riches I ask, but awe.

From

The Red Line

1992

DAWN

At the day camp years ago where we drove
from the projects to an outlying municipal park, .
the trees were so lush, the kids didn't know
what to do with that soft filtered light,
so unlike raw sun blasting the sidewalks.
They'd glare, spin out a wisecracking jive,

or hide their faces against a trunk, gouging
the bark. One of the tough girls, eight years old,
high octane mouth, called me *Kotex breath*,
then flopped in my lap. Sweat made her dark skin
iridescent. See them birds? she asked, leaning back.
She went to the country once, on a bus, to visit

her grandfather and he had all kinds of birds,
craziest racket you ever heard. We watched a few
fuss in and out of the leaves, catching light
on their wings, light making everything its own color,
so we couldn't tell bird wing from jiggling leaf,
and I totally believed we were all connected. Only

I wasn't thinking just then about trash in the street,
or crumbling blacktop, or what it's like to climb
twelve flights in the dark through that pissy smell,
the sound of feet rushing up behind.
That afternoon while the top branches caught
some barely translatable breeze, I couldn't answer

when all this poured out and she put it to me—
how come, how come? Instead I traced letters
on her back for her to guess, this little girl
who the next day didn't show, and when she did
wouldn't speak to me, so I don't know what
to say about the hardness she came to,

whether it was wrong or right, I just remember
her back shaking in spasms as she threw those
rocks, making the water fly up and shine a minute
before it disappeared, her back which had jerked
itself away from me, as if to say—You are useless,
you don't know, you don't know a thing.

THE COAT

I stare at the blue linoleum
while my mother grieves for her lost sister,
not dead, just more trashed than usual—
my aunt, I suddenly recall from years ago,
sunk to her knees on this floor

begging my uncle to go to the Red Lion
for another bottle of Scotch, then going
herself, in high heels, on the cindery
shoulder of the road, tear streaks through powder
on her face, wearing a real leopard coat.

She came back, pine needles and leaves stuck
to her shoes, cradling the bottle, baby-
talking to my mother who chopped onions
and didn't look up, my uncle who stared at
the news. *What's going on?* I must have asked

and nobody answered, so I turned it
over in my mind, the swirls in that coat,
the streaks on her face, her red plastic jangle
of bracelets, till once, in college, I woke
with a headache, nauseous, and thought: leaning

from arm to arm, into those huge faces,
Oh, that's who I was last night. Now I hear
that at a barbecue in Shore Acres,
beside those black glassy lagoons, she got
so drunk she called my mother, *Joan, Joan,*

the name of her daughter, poked slurred advice
into my mother's chest, grabbed her as she
tried to pull away, so they both nearly
fell into the hot grill. I can imagine
my mother's face, patient, sad, turned slightly,

too careful to actually say, *Aren't you
ashamed?* My aunt spills her drink on the grill,
laughs—what the hell—lights the wrong end
of a cigarette, and in the sudden stench
and flare, I picture their two faces

like different answers to the same question,
as if for years each thought—if *she* is right,
then *I* am terribly wrong, each looking
at herself in the other's mirror. What was
the question? My mother doesn't remember.

It was my aunt who described how their father
would come home glowering, not speak for days,
not raise his voice, or touch them. Just glare
till their skin felt like sieves. My mother learned
to stare off to the side, closed in her own thoughts,

while my aunt kept looking, asking, *What did
I do?* with that way she jiggles her head,
as if listening so hard something has to
explode. Maybe that's it. I've seen her fling
her arms as she talks, so liquor splashes

against the wall. She gets louder as night
goes on, not wanting to know when it might
start again—the silence, perhaps, the glare.
I've seen a chair slip out from under her,
her clatter against the wall, knocking down

pictures. *Who did that?* she wags her head,
blaming a table or rug, then the faces
pointing at her. And maybe she's right—
how can a family let just one person
wear all the scars? I didn't live with glares,

but with such tight, restrained voices,
plenty of times I've put on that coat
the color of sunlight on Scotch, its burning
swirl of black eyes. I've put on the fear
as evening begins to teeter and slide,

that ash on the tip of a cigarette
bobbing in somebody's mouth, ash on the grill
she knocks over, kicks across the white
pebbled ground. *You all right?* they rush up,
and I feel skinless too in their hands,

tightening to steady her as she blurs from
face to face, trying to decide the answer—
whether to throw back her head and roar,
or just close her eyes and slip through them,
their stupid miserable questions.

PICK A CARD

I wonder if it still exists—Point Pleasant boardwalk,
Jenkinson's Pavilion, old people rocking
deaf dumb and blind. Light blubs flashing around
roulette wheels. If I blotted myself from the scene,
would the tide rush into the empty space? Or would there be
this jagged hole in the picture around which the water does its
break-and-be-healed, break-and-be-healed
routine, a photographic trick?

Couples strolling the long pier that night years ago
must have looked down and thought we were just kissing.
But that man's kiss split my lip, realigned my vision
into a tilting martini glass on the Rip Tide sign going
pink-green, pink-green, getting no place. I saw
how useless it was to try.

This morning when sleep finally settled down, folding itself
back out of me like wings, and I woke with heavy ankles,
a stiff neck, I was remembering against my will
that night summers and miles away, when I felt my arm
twist till I thought it would break, felt two fingers
force open my mouth . . .

To shake it off, I went to the community center
overlooking the harbor, was assigned the boy with the low IQ
who knows only one card trick, though he knows that well.
I settled in for a long afternoon of flash cards, Old Maid,
Go Fish. And watching that pale soft boy whose face could
not be dissuaded from shining, I imagined he materialized

from a mother walking home counting her tips, a father
in a ski mask flashing a knife. How far he must have
traveled to arrive at simple delight. He made me want
everything inside me that's been speeding on anger
to slow down and fall away, like this harbor after hours
when the cranes and dredging machines stop agitating
and water has a chance to be heard.

I can't possibly piece it all together, but I know that
for a long time after sitting with this unfinished boy
I'll be making lists of who to forgive. I'll be realizing
I don't know the first thing, after watching his mother
so tender with her fingers in his hair, hearing her tell me
there was not a better hand she was cheated out of.
The boy doesn't know much, but he can tell by her open face
that he's done something well, so he does it again.
Pick a card, any card.

A SMALL PATCH OF ICE

If I told you we could see nail polish stopping
a run in one skater's tights, a safety pin
in a zipper, that their patch of ice was the size
of my kitchen, no room to leap or spin—you might
agree with my daughter hissing fiercely, *Let's go.*
All they do is circle to tinny music, then stop
in a flourish of shaved ice. But the little mist
that makes reminds me of the gray flickering light
in those films where you come to care about
a balding aerialist, a clown weeping back stage,
the way they'll talk later in their van, in French
or Italian, with subtitles, about despair.

Maybe that's why I linger. Or is it the smell
of popcorn and cotton candy mixed with machine oil
from a hand-pushed Zamboni—the smell of boardwalks
from childhood, neck-jerk rides, tiered rows of teacups
you toss quarters into, those wiry barkers with burnt
cheekbones, voices snatching at your back—Hey, girl
in pink shorts. So we stay to the end.
Then while I scrape a thin crust of ice off
the windshield, my daughter says: *If you can't
do it right, you shouldn't do it at all.*
She's just seen the Olympics on TV and
doesn't like to think how far from grace things

can fall, or how most of us just circle and trudge,
like these skaters, in boots and jeans now, lugging
the heavy ice frame, the clunky machines out to
the U-Haul behind their van. Soon they'll doze,
or bitch, or razz each other about who gets the seat
by the wheel well. Someone will let out a long sigh
settling in by the window, longing for what
we call "the real thing"—the kind of ice you need
to work out fast and hard. In those movies, sometimes
the hard pressure of facing just how far we are
from our dreams turns someone kinky and wise,
fills the screen with pungent images we remember

for years—the sweep of birds across a square,
clown suit hanging on a line. I'm telling you this
because my daughter doesn't want to hear it.
She doesn't want to know those boardwalks
were full of legless men, I guess from the war,
and one leaned toward me, an anchor tattooed
on his arm where his rolled up sleeve cradled
a pack of smokes. A stub of a man, with apish arms,
he jiggled a cigarette in my face, the way someone
does with a bone to make a dog come. *Girlie,*
he whispered as I ran off, and what good would it do
to tell my daughter there's grace in falling too,

in that guy starting after me on his crutches
with huge strides like an ungainly bird that might
actually take off, or the way he threw back
his head and laughed—so loud I still see him
on those thin stilts in the middle of the boardwalk
flustering parents so they grab their kids
and step wide around him. I was twelve then,
the age my daughter is now, and maybe it isn't
cruel to believe you'll never get so wounded
or shoddy. Maybe to grow at all we have to
pretend they have nothing to do with us,
these dark pleasures, this dinky patch of ice.

SEX ED

Well-dressed, demure, jammed into those
politely arranged desks, it's hard to be
serious, but we are. No one even parts lips
to acknowledge what used to drive us crazy
in the back seats of cars, what kept us up
half the night reliving the last slow dance,
girl on her toes, guy bent at the knees
to press in against her.

The instructors speak precisely about
the importance of our children knowing the facts,
so surely none of us in our high heels and
neck ties is going to admit how our first mistakes
have suddenly blossomed so tender and lovely
we've been forgiven a thousand times,
a thousand times forgiven and repeated ourselves.

But fingering the graffiti on this desk,
I remember being braille to you, being read
like a steamy novel, and how those lessons
stayed with us, practical as driver's ed, those hours
of simulation behind the wheel of a parked car.
The truth is I don't regret having studied with you,
though I do feel inarticulate, like an athlete
asked to speak in a room of kids, who has nothing
to say except, "practice, practice."

Once our daughter watched the cat in heat
yowl and slither across the floor, and without
looking up asked, would that happen to her. Sometimes
it isn't shame that makes us speechless. It's not
regret that makes me linger at the curb watching
her toss back her yellow hair and yank open
the heavy doors to school.

144 MINDEN STREET

I can still see him from down the block, my landlord, Charlie,
in sleeveless T-shirt—the kind with ribs we called
guinea tuxedos in high school, when Italians were all we had.
My old landlord in a shirt so yellow it's begging
his daughter-in-law to come take the laundry,

still stands on what's left of the front porch, cigar
in mouth, heaving gray sighs through the spring air.
He's been watching the purveyors of loss
take over the block, jabbering their unsavory tongues,
wearing glasses to further darken the streets which have

already daunted his daughter-in-law. She's elegant,
one of those whose car does not entrust itself
to our curb. I've never seen her, only bleached hair
through the tinted glass of a black car arriving bimonthly
to take the old man to dinner in the burbs, where presumably

emotion's recollected in tranquility,
not amplified, like the car doing *La Cucaracha*,
taking the corner on two wheels, which one night abruptly
docked itself under our house. It was cause for celebration
in the ghetto night—two guys saved by a hair and the beer

that relaxed them. But no number of dudes
saying, Be cool, old man, could stop Charlie
from hyperventilating over that hood jammed into our steps.
Such fate, he sighed, to survive Hitler and end up here.
If those fools had seen what I've seen, he started the next day.

And I should have said—What, Charlie, what?
Would they sober up, learn English? Are you telling me
you didn't see more than was good for you? Are you telling me
you've had anything good to say about life after Hitler?
Look, Charlie, at our fancy neighbor, in his handsome suit,

tumbling on the lawn with his sons: two guns
in leather holsters strapped to his chest and we know
he doesn't work for the cops. You'll be dead, Charlie,
before I can argue that, when the Feds move in, he'll up
the insurance and pay to have it burned—

the octagonal crib he's so proud of,
the enormous fish tank embedded in the wall—
all of it, Charlie, starting with oily rags in the hallway,
then chunks of roof glowing as thy hit the street
and spatter like water balloons—everything we think

he's working so hard for in his own gangsterish way.
Charlie, you think I know nothing, but I'm going
to survive you. I'm going to stand here after you're gone,
leaning on the call box, looking at our new unpainted steps,
and resume this conversation, telling you—Don't leave.

You'll go nuts at your daughter-in-law's, won't last six months.
Here, at least you can go out strong, hold the floor, filibuster
on losing. Losing, Charlie, as if there's another way.
I'm watching the one tree on the block that survived the fire,
send its useless green tears all over the street,

wishing I had said to you then, in that piss-poor moment
so vivid in my mind: Don't leave us. There's nothing to climb,
the stairs are broken. That phone ringing on the third floor—
it's probably a wrong number, someone confusing us again
with the Boston ballet.

FORGET YOUR LIFE

After Rumi

Plaster drips from the ceiling.
You close your eyes and think, *skylight*.
All night you jackhammer through asphalt,
but in the morning the surface resumes unchanged
and people drive nonchalantly to work.
So what good is thinking about God
when it doesn't blow the tiles off the roof
or buckle the street, heaving up layers
of sandstone beneath the city?

Steam from the molten rocks of elementary
textbooks taught you how things squeeze
to a boil in the center of earth. You've been
squinting ever since, clenching your jaw,
at war with yourself, two deaf mutes
constantly jabbing. One of whom proclaims,
God is Great! The other doesn't so much disagree
as think that's the trouble.

It takes a certain kind of violence
to wrench yourself free. A certain shock
to make you quit talking and give that helpless
shrug, the first step in a dance that turns
faster and faster. Even accountants get dizzy
and wad up their checks. Even philosophers
begin to laugh.

Don't be surprised to find yourself walking close
to the edge of a dock and suddenly tripping,
unable to keep your fists jammed in your pockets.

There's a whole school of ragged children
lined up on the riverbank. Look how heavy
the mistrustful ones are. They lift their feet
and drop straight down. Each day now
I say this to myself: Forget your life.
Prayer is a different use of words, not those
frantic splashes demanding so much help no one can get near.

Don't go to work. Call in sick, or not
sick but desperate. You've been trying too hard
to unearth the perfect student, one who reads
so intently all her rough opinions leave her
like swine rushing over a cliff. Now, teach yourself.

THREE DEATHS

Last autumn, tensed for winter, I was sealing up
windows, wrapping shrubs in burlap. I never thought of spring,
never considered putting those cold bulbs in the ground.

But outside the halfway house, under moonlight,
my nephew, possessed by growing delusions, carefully sowed what
resembled to him shrunken heads, the dark insides of a scream.

And my friend, in brief remission, waved me away
with my solemn worry while she kneeled in the rain cold
garden, emaciated, hairless, white as bone. *It's grim enough,*
she hissed, trying to whistle.

November, December, January, she wrote letters
about accepting what we're given. *This isn't passivity,*
she said. *I've come to see I've been given a lot.*

February, my nephew's garbled note read,
where I'm going knives don't exist, pianos and doors
will not rise up against me: *Rejoice, my friends.*

But now it is March, and the graveyard is full of these
trumpets and flares. I don't bother to read the stones
because this month every one is my father's, whose voice
I try to remember and can't.

He didn't leave me a single word, though I did hear him laugh.
I have pictures of him leaning on a fence
like a mirthful grasshopper chewing tobacco:

Busy, busy, busy, he seems to chide the diligent ants,
my father, who when he knew he would die, licked the flap
of a manila envelope bearing my name in which he had placed

such strange advice: four pennies hammered into a tea set,
a monkey carved out of peach it, assorted puzzles, key rings,
a whistle shaped like a tiny violin.

Don't Explain

BEHIND THE SAINT-LAZARE STATION

After the photograph by Henri Cartier-Bresson

Every day, seventh period, we'd look
at the photo over the teacher's desk,
till the word RAILOWSKY on the station wall
started a whole year of fake Polish,
perfected by a boy we called Joe
Needs-A-Whiskey. I can still see him posed
under the principal's glare: open shirt,
greased hair, a sullen Elvis. But in art class,
bent over his sketch pad, a softer Joe:
face slack, lost in concentration,

the way the photographer must have
forgotten himself behind that station
waiting for a perfect moment—caught,
as a man leaped off a prone ladder
into a rain-flooded lot, the water
doubling him in a sort of pas de deux.
And if the runner himself merely passed
through, his best moment occurring almost
without him? Well, it's an argument
I first heard from Joe, whistling Doo Wop

through his teeth, as he quick-sketched the page,
hardly looking at his hands. That's how
the photo was snapped, as if from inside,
photographer swept up in the man's run
across the ladder, the water repeating
his leap, dancers in the poster taking off
with it across the station wall. How'd you
do that? I'd sigh, after a swirling hand
and some off-key "Earth Angel" became
a wine bottle and pears on folds of cloth,

while my measured lines kept ending up
erasure smears tossed in the basket,
cartoon bottles I couldn't sweat into roundness.
That whole year I lingered in art class
long after the bell, not knowing why,
never expecting those moments to last—
Joe squinting over my crumpled sketches
for a shadow or line to like, taking
my stiff hand in his, scent of nicotine
and graphite, as we moved Ouija-like

across the page. English, math—anywhere
outside that room, you could follow the rules,
get somewhere. But there was Joe. There was this
photo saying, What's a straight line? What's time?
At the top of the ladder, we just kept
climbing, Joe riding my hand all over
the paper, across state lines. *Girlchik,*
he'd say, *we need a whiskey,* and he'd draw
till we were loose and giddy, as if we
had drunk whatever he put in my hand.

MISTERIOSO

If you jiggle the book of Russian icons
the cloth on God's knees shimmers like the suit
Thelonious Monk wears in *Straight No Chaser*—
sharkskin shifting as he leans into the keys
picking up shadow and light—almost grooved

like those old Cracker Jacks cards giving us
two scenes we could jiggle back and forth:
a boy's smile flipping into a scowl, the world
notched and mutable—or in another light
a child might assume whatever was playing

on a person's face, there was an opposite
lurking behind. And that's just how it is,
my friend would say, we're both sides of the coin,
head and tail pressed, the way in the movie,
Monk rasps a few unintelligible words,

then sits down to his bright clear riffs, their jab
and dodge against the dark—without which,
my friend insists, what's light? It's how
the mystics argue too: the soul just a rumor,
expensive perfume sealed in a flask,

until it's broken. This same friend once felt
her life wasn't worth two bits. She downed
a bottle of pills, then walked, hoping to drop
unknown, no wallet, just a stiff in the morgue.
But God must have had different plans—

otherwise, she can't explain how the spare change
in her pocket, embossed head on a coin
under her thumb, made her feel her daughter's
real face swollen by grief. It got her to a cop.
Doctors emptied her out—years of loathing

finally gone. And the world came back
pure gift. She told me this when I was stuck
in a hard-luck story of my own, same side
coming up no matter how I flipped: loss
still loss, heartbreak still hoarding itself,

playing its rot-gut tunes no matter what
buttons I pushed. Which is why I love Monk,
who makes of the past such variations
in the confession booth of my car,
it's as if a tune's not a tune until it's stretched

more ways than you'd think it could go
without snapping. And when he snaps it,
what can you do but say *yes* to all that
discord and delay, those runs and aversions
you had to be hurt into hearing?

BLUES IS MY COMPANION

I

On the radio, Eddie Kirkland, bluesman, talking
with a deejay about the road—long string
of one-nighters, then Sunday mornings driving

through small towns, folks gathering for church . . .
Once he pulled off the road with his guitar,
started strumming, and it seemed a whole woods

full of birds, who'd been making the craziest racket,
hushed right up. Half the morning he tested it—
man sing, bird hush, man still, bird squawk like mad.

Says he could live off that a long time. *Eddie,*
Eddie Kirkland, ladies and gentlemen—the deejay
starts a tape, and it's blues you can dance to.

You have to put down your paring knife and move.
Dinner can wait. You have to tear out time
and place, tape it to the wall, newsprint

photo of his face, tilted back in light, all sweat
and gleam. Forget black & white, forget history
with its great divides, its SWAT team of assumptions

swarming in. Here's mystery, ladies and gentlemen.
Plays an upbeat blues, town after no-name town.
Says he just lets the music bubble and smoke,

till all those tired folk can't help but dance.
Mississippi to Chicago—carried him
sixty years, in and out of trouble, in and out

of war, rotgut, Jim Crow, those steel-string hungry,
those battered, hocked, rebought—those backroom
to spotlight, sweet, get-up Child, blues.

II

For years I wouldn't turn on the radio,
wouldn't let any kind of music get
to me, after growing up with my sister

who breathed it, drank it like soda—music,
instead of movies, guys, the phone, whatever
the rest of us were using for flotation.

I hated the way we'd be talking, I'd
be getting to the juicy part, then
suddenly she'd tilt her head so I knew

what was coming: *Shhh, shhh,* and whatever
I was whispering (sobbing)—"the teacher said
she'd flunk me," "then he put his hand on my—"

was nothing. What was the something she heard
instead? I couldn't tell, I'd be so backed up
with the choked-off sentence, the words like phlegm.

(Can you just swallow them? Don't they have to
go somewhere?) When I caught my breath, blinked,
there she'd be raising and lowering the trap

door to the attic, unfolding it's scratchy creak
and spring, elongating then snapping the pitch.
Or she'd be off to the keyboard, sounding

one note, a handful maybe, as if she'd caught
only a small riff of it herself, just a breath
of this half-heard thing. I hated the way

it was always more important than
my story, her great pneumatic hush,
that cathedral door shutting in my face.

III

But there's a moment in a B. B. King song
the guitar holds a note, then the sax comes in,
same pitch, and keeps going higher

as the guitar falls away. "Sweet sixteen,
and you wouldn't do nothing for me."
Every time it comes round on the tape,

say I'm jogging, something hushes inside,
gets clarified—something I hadn't known
was jumbled. Low-down words, it's true,

but then music takes over, lament
pushing out of lechery into loss
so palpable it fills the body, the song

plugged into a communal dirge—like birds
lifted out of territory and hunger,
given rest from their frenzy. *Frenzy?*

Would they suddenly see it that way?
Dull ordinary brown birds in the shade,
until the music flushes them into

the most amazing sun-struck indigo.
"When I lost my baby I found the blues
instead." You can live off that a long time

if you have to, the way on live recordings
an old singer will sometimes clear his throat
so you can feel the knot in yours,

feel it pass through—a pushed-down,
kind of stepped-on thing at the back of the song.

HOOD

I can still see the hand-painted signs
on ghetto fences: *Keep Out, Attack Dog,*
and just enough of them not bluffing
it must have given our gangster neighbor

the idea: his own loping Great Dane
one of those. So, paper bag over his head,
he jabbed a broomstick into the dog's chest
again and again, as if her whimpers enraged him,

and that combined dog-cry, man-howl
filled the block like thick industrial smoke.
In goes the meanness, *out* goes the baffled hurt
of her yelps, or so he must have reasoned.

But what's reason to a dog, who just likes
dirt cool on her belly, likes a tight squeeze
through the fence, the sudden fragrance
of a neighbor's garden? What is reason

to her unwary joy, who licked crumbs
off our fingers, followed mailmen and cops
down the block, racing ahead, trotting back
for a rub? He must have thought it out:

that broom, the bag hiding his face.
But when he lunged, putting his whole body
into each jab, did another argument take over:
blood smell, old rage, a cornered hood

turning on what he loves, or loving only
that turn, the snap of another's will?
I can still hear those bewildered yips,
as if the dog, trembling in her pen,

just couldn't get the next part
of the lesson we were hearing
all over the block: first hurt, then fear,
then the clenched heart's furious growl.

———

66

A KIND OF DARKNESS

Butterflies—those sailboats of the insect world,
serene among engine gunners, like our best thoughts
rising without fuel, free of ambition's guzzle.

But once, jogging an old farm road, I saw
a rabbit carcass swarmed by yellow wings
nibbling, sniffing, not budging when I stomped,

the way in some parts of town figures huddle
to pass a needle or pipe, so starved for it
not even flashing lights disperse their concentration.

Imagine—those frail Velcro mouths wolf-hungry,
flitting from death to death, the way I used to
fear my grandmother's wet kisses, pressed

from lip to lip, would spread old age.
She died, one whole side of her body purple
from the fall, a grimace stiffened on her face

the undertaker had to hammer out.
I can hardly stand the thought that her longed-for
afterlife wasn't all floating clouds and praise,

but a moment of throat-locked suffocation,
and then—Hieronymus Bosch! Maybe I didn't see
those bright petal-thin wings on the dead rabbit,

maybe the twist in my grandmother's face
was more like the sirening howl karate choppers
let out striking a pile of bricks—say the wall

between *this* world and *that,* as if heaven's
a realm so strange it's only entered by force.
The year we moved north to the city,

we asked our young daughter what she missed most,
and butterflies flew from her mouth—yellow,
orange, black and white, striped and plain, blue ones too.

Then a sigh, and *purple,* she cried, stomping off,
leaving us helpless against that mystic garden
forming in her mind, its tale of banishment and loss.

Maybe it wasn't for her we dug out the book
showing how purple exists—under crisp tissues,
in such frail powdery glitter, it's as if

the crushed wings of a real one had been reformed
on the page. Natural habitat: Cameroon, Brazil,
and that bright world always flickering at the edge

of sight, that iridescence sunlight makes
out of dust on wings, out of anything distant,
while *here* is a kind of darkness we tear at.

FINE ARTS

Riding a backpack through the museum, my son
would cry up the scale from suggestion to howl—
his first staccato sentence: *down, out, home, now.*
Was it that gallery of stern grandparents he couldn't
grin into sweet babblers? We'd hardly get

past them to Degas or Toulouse-Lautrec
without a guard ushering us out. Never made it
to mummies, stiff as a game of statues
gone horribly wrong, without the bum's rush
to the lawn, where my boy happily waddled up

to cigarette butts and crumpled wrappers,
chased pigeons into flight, or tried to catch light
playing through leaves. Light in long shafts,
or high noon's neon—isn't that what painters love?
Sometimes after a snack, we'd try again,

rushing past ballerinas in pink, slumped on break
or stretching at the bar, torch singers in fishnet,
one calf exposed, so you can almost hear
a man's whiskey laugh, music pulsing the floor.
Then *out, now, down, home* would rise again,

and like art thieves, we'd duck the guards,
slipping into a crowd, past a tour guide's phrase,
marvelous instant. We'd snatch what we could
and make off—enough to see trolley tracks gleam,
or make a lone pigeon seem Picasso's invention.

And a whole flock? My boy would crane
to follow their swoop and rush till he toppled over,
learning the world's worth falling for,
not a bad place. On the steps there'd be
bigger boys with free passes scanning

the crowd for fake parents to shuffle them in,
as if art's guardians didn't trust them alone
in the basement Egyptian rooms, art's guardians
intent on making sure something that's outlived
almost unscathed, Aristotle, Suleiman,

Einstein, will outlive these boys as well.
Such an old debate: those who long to finger
mummy rags, or after the day at school want
to pencil, "Sue was here" on anything in sight—
versus—the guards with their "Mustn't disturb,"

as if they never saw how light in one mood
paints us gold and in the next just wants to
obliterate. What's a mother to do
but tell her son, if he wants home, it's his,
and if some spendthrift years lead through *down*

& *out*, through whiskey rush and throaty song?
Well, she'll tell herself that's not the end
of anything—after this *now*, there's another,
another marvelous instant, we're far
from closing, far from whatever that means.

MONKEY HOUSE

Such a howl went up when I walked in,
big lippy kisses and hoots so loud
I couldn't help but turn. Then as I stepped away,
wails, head clobbering. We did that
over and over—kiss-kiss and head-conk—
barely noticing the crowd. I never saw
such hairy grief, big knuckled loneliness
scraping the floor. *Closer,*

he motioned, *closer*—just the opposite
of my humanoid family, those dreary
worriers, who'd like to zap out of the genes
any feeling that can't sit like a lady,
keep its elbows off the table. Stuff it back in
and stay calm, they insist, or we'll all be
hurled down dark eons, back into furry faces
and curled toes, shitting on floors.

I started pacing in front of the cage,
a one-person house of hysterics. Other visitors
carefully tip-toed around. The chimp lay
on his back, picked his toes, pursed his great
flexible lips, and I was about to say: my people
didn't use words, they did it with eyebrows, tiny
sucked-in breaths, obsessive as painting on grains
of rice with brushes made from one split hair—

but then I looked up at his body, its big
furry smarts, the way whatever he did
he did completely, reaching an arm behind
his head to get to his chin, fizzing his face up
like a seltzer bottle. "You feel what you feel,"
I said, and he rolled his eyes, looking
everywhere but at me, as if to say,
"Interview over. You got what you came for."

And suddenly he was limp, slumped over,
as though a grief too big to thump or shriek
had dropped down on his shoulders, a sorrow
cut deep over what's become of his kind.
I put my palms to the glass where his had been,
as if I could feel the rough pads of his fingers,
a trace of that heat meant for a whole jungle
now crammed into one very small house.

FALLING

When the house began to tip, I stepped back,
trying to save it, or me, or both. Was it wrong
to climb the ladder rungs nailed to the trunk,
to squeeze through porthole plank rot?
Should I have stayed on the ground, not leaned
toward the river's meandering flash
I wouldn't have known was there?
How could I have known that brief leafy
diversion would fling me out, door
after random extravagant door,
thick shingles of green tearing, green
hinges snapping, broken off from the rest
and frozen in my mind, so again and again,
for months, in traffic or on the edge of sleep,
I am let loose and flailing, finding myself
on the verge, almost bird in the brief
clumsy flight a fall is before landing.
I have seen little birds drop straight down
as if their wings were glued, and I have seen
old movies where they play a jump backward
to trick us, and succeed, because who doesn't
want to soar, to rise in reverse up
ladders of air? But to get there
we'd have to enter the teetering house,
let go when we want most to hold on,
want *up* so badly we refuse the *down*
it's made of, the whole clattering drop.
And what of the other world, invisible
to this, glimpsed a split second in the river's
quicksilver through branches, a flicker
on the edge of thought, and gone?
Could I have flown there and plucked a twig,
could I have healed the tumbling house?
The man who loves me and watched
from outside says he still trembles seeing me
draped rag-limp over the wrecked sill,

says he thought he was watching my death,
and don't call it by another name.
But could death really be that green,
the river's flickering gleam
and those little birds in their plain brown wrappers
who just before crash flash their wings,
vanishing through a hedge of light?

FOUR CROWS AT DUSK

Perched on a steep slate roof: the first—
God knows what it wants, all squawk,
like it's deaf and has to shout remarks
about a blonde in short-shorts, a couple
kissing in the street, motorcycle revving.

The second's got an itch it can't quite reach,
so it bites and yanks, wing stuck out
like a banging shutter. Number three
doesn't like its position, hops to the end—
no better. Hops back, shimmies its tail,

drops something. More glob than bird,
the squawker's quiet now, as if it ran down
mid-sentence, having made the same point
thirty years. The preener is calm too, spent,
like a sob subsiding. The last one sits

and stares, turns its head now and then,
or you wouldn't even know it was a bird.
You'd think maybe a tired bowtie,
or a black, half-wilted rose. Not one
of four crows on a steep church roof

starting to crumble—till it flies off,
leaving three, and a little girl on a big-wheel
not answering when her mother hollers
from an upstairs window, "You're gonna
get it, I'm gonna whip your butt": three,

and the other on a wire now, call and response
blacking out those threats, so the child keeps
clattering down the block. Bad girl birds,
raspy voices in your head—"Way to go, kid.
Hot damn"—as if every gripe, every flash

of rage you thought you'd regret takes the stage
now in a gospel quartet, the four black-robed
survival sisters—half-hoarse soloist at the mic,
wailing her been-through-the-fire, got-burnt,
but-it-ain't-over-yet-honey good news.

SPARROWS

1

My neighbor's tree was simmering,
a spruce bubbling over with chirps, louder
than the city garbage truck idling at the curb,

louder than my own mind saying, "Those guys
think you're nuts." Or my other mind asking,
"How can you ignore the music boiling in this tree?"

So I shook the long green sleeves of its branches,
hoping to see that song's belly and wings,
its little wiry feet, to flush out those notes

jumping through dense staves, those quick
flickering heartbeats pulsing from limb to limb.
I know people get struck for this, some wisdom

can cost fingers or eyes. We get sent back
to some place very old, where things are only
half-converted, earth clods still clinging to roots,

mouths clotted with beard hair and consonants.
There, a tree is more than a tree, still part-god,
knowing things, screeching when cut.

Even the cross weeps then, a bitter speech,
baring its soul. The truck idled, clusters
of junior high kids made an elaborate ritual

out of snapping Zippos, taking long drags,
but there was a door I could close on that,
I could squeeze between branches, press against

the trunk, letting those birds bite—that's what
I imagined—the birds yanking my hair, the mouths
that made the music, making music out of me.

2

But I was afraid of that wanting, afraid
of the way wanting I don't even know I have
sometimes leaks from my face, so a stranger

out of nowhere will offer a smoke.
Is it just a matter of degrees between him & me,
and the crazy woman who walks our streets,

gesturing wildly—her arms all leathery tendon,
as if the desire she's vagrant with is flight,
her body a semaphore, coaxing down spirits

or fending them off. The birds were quiet now.
I wanted to chase them out, to see how many
and what kind. I wanted their music all over me

like mosquito bites, swarming the way in sci fi movies
a sound can make you writhe on the ground.
Perhaps they'd think I *was* the tree and get impatient

with hiding—small grayish birds, dozens of them,
sparrows maybe. I wanted to hold one in my hand,
its fierce panic fluttering through me.

Isn't the afterlife full of creatures who think like this—
that fox, for instance, who jumps and jumps at grapes
dangling just out of reach. He'd probably like

a fat little sparrow, then a rain puddle to rinse
the feathers from his mouth. And what if God
is listening right now? What if God is thinking,

"Give her what she wants," so suddenly
my arms are green, my legs hard and shaggy,
impossible to move. When does it go too far?

———

3

Music and desire, that spontaneous combustion—
I half-remember a man crouched in a belfry
and ringers tugging the heavy ropes:

down they pull, and up they're lifted, as one
after another, huge bell after lumbering bell
swings and tolls, and the poor fellow grips his head,

collapses, blood trickling from his ears . . . One side
of my mind takes this as proof: "Salt, stone,
straitjacket for you." But the other also threatens:

"You already are stone, if you don't get close
to that music." So it goes, the yammering debate.
Meanwhile, the tree frays and sparks like hot wires,

sound spatters and pours. Not ache or longing—
that's us, pulling the limbs, hoping to be lifted.
For them it must be all arrival, pure *here here*

now here, a flock of tongueless flames splashing out
like sterno, and nothing's charred. The spruce
is young, but still it's been standing a long time

with nothing but the usual wind, rain, sun, until now.
Nothing? Usual? That was my first mistake.
And I didn't know how long it could take,

standing, pricked by those branches, trying to see
the music, or the plump purple light of grapes,
or the sad eyes of the crazy woman the junior high kids

love to tease—to see and not grasp, but be grasped,
to stand here whether anything flickers, bursts
lit and singing from the tree, or nothing does.

DON'T EXPLAIN

I just wanted to tell what I saw—
a brown river, the Raritan, sprinkled
with loosestrife petals, two cassette tapes
dangling from a high bridge, rippled and looping
like kite strings in the wind—but questions came in:
What was the music, snagged on dirty heads,
tossed from a car speeding over the bridge?
And since my father went to school here, could he
have stood at this culvert, stripping petals
into the river? Back then, did flocks of geese
trample the bank down to stark red clay?
Over the phone, Mother says, *Oh sure, sure,*
to the brown water, to loosestrife and geese,
Oh sure, the way she'd answer years ago
when I asked, Did they have cars back then? trains?
records? Later there were questions I didn't ask,
darker things—Did you know the same years you were
in school, Billie Holiday was scrubbing floors
in a whorehouse, playing Louis Armstrong
on an old Victrola? That would make Mother wince.
Ditto, if I asked, Were you ever so mad
you could've ripped out your favorite tape
and hurled it, so mad you half understand
the video—Woodstock redux—Nine Inch Nails
out-Hendrixing Hendrix, destroying something
they love *and* hate, yanking the keyboard
from its sockets, smashing guitar on amp,
again and again till only the drummer's
left, ducking hurled mics—God.
I wanted to say wind unraveled those tapes
like an aria too beautiful to be heard,
so we have to imagine the song we'd play
till it wore out, then carry on inside us, wound
on spools of feeling that could spin it to mind any time.
That's what my dead father was to me—on a reel
for my comfort, better than life, till the night
I sat up reading in his own hand, letters
full of slurs, doors he wanted shut against

just about everyone. All night as I read,
my old tape slowed to the indecipherable
rumble of dead batteries and I ripped it out.
Though maybe it snagged on some undergirding
in my mind and still hangs, now limp, now billowing,
inaudible aftermath of rage, small lull
in the music, which lasts a while till something
shakes it up—the way two joggers saw me
on the culvert and just had to shout, *Don't jump,
ha ha*. Balance almost begs for that,
as if whatever made my father so intent
on closing doors is what makes us now want
to hear the voices that were shut out, want
to rewind and play again the band hurling
instruments and mics, dumping water buckets
on the crowd dancing in a lumbered frenzy,
young kids lost in the song, whipping their heads
so wet hair stings their faces, feeling part of
the muddy ground, not caring where the crowd
carries them as long as they're moving. And now
the static and screech—is this my father's lost voice
singing inside me, *The world's going down. And down*—
me singing back—*in order to rise?* Down
to where no one's shut out, down to the riverbank's
bare red clay, down to a voice like Holiday's,
that even on a bad tape made from old records,
sends her losses straight to the marrow—*Don't Explain,
Strange Fruit*—voice totally shot by the end,
as if the life couldn't be kept out,
the music couldn't keep itself from breaking.

REDBUD

I had to step outside, having just finished
the letters of Keats, who for all his talk of easeful death
told his friend Brown he wanted to live, wanted his *feeling*
for light and shade, his memories of walking with her—
everything reminds him. *Oh God! God! God!—*
he was barely able to write it, *I should have had her*
when I was in health. Does that mean what it sounds like to us?
Window light and leaf shade on the porch. Next door,
people slipping into their coats, leaving a party. *See ya, Take it easy.*
Hard to believe just last week, I looked up to see a blue truck
crest the hill, flying it seemed, and the driver's surprised eyes
as he fishtailed into me. Barely time to ask, *Am I going to die?*
But nobody did, so can I say it was worth it? say that *beauty*
totaled my car?—the stand of redbuds I'd gone to see, purple blossoms
on rain-slick limbs, stark as petals on a painted scroll blooming
above waterfalls, above tiny figures on a foot bridge crossing
a steep gorge. There we were, waiting for a trooper in that fellow's cab,
and it seemed he had to tell how he got caught cheating his boss
at the stables, how he was planning to leave a whole mess
of bad credit, racing stubs, a woman who finally said, *Get out.*
Beauty must have been a kind of charm he knew how to use,
aqua eyes, easy smile, the way he could tell his scam and still run it,
share a thermos, ask ideas for his new name. All around us, those redbuds
so stunning I can't remember now if he drugged a horse,
or fixed a race, dealt off the bottom with his fine jittery hands.
I had Keats in my pocket, himself worried about money,
walking through Scotland to see its waterfalls, astonished
by what he hadn't imagined, the subtleties of tone—moss, rock-weed—
I live in the eye he says to his brother. But they're gone—
Keats, Fanny, Tom, everyone he wrote those exuberant letters to.
What good is *beauty?* Still I saw it, those redbuds, like the moment
making love, into the rush of it, when you think, *I could die now.*
After which—the truck, that fellow telling the trooper flat out
he was doing 50 in a 25, as if beauty has to press its luck,
which the insurance company said had run out:
We'll get him, don't you worry. I don't.

Because he's gone, among the tossing heads of horses,
their nervous sidesteps—gone, without a name,
like those tiny figures dissolving in paint. Imagine,
standing over a gorge where a waterfall plummets—lost,
not so much in thought as its graceful absence, so lost
there is nothing else to want from the world. The *world*.
How beautiful the word sounds. *Whorled*. Purple blossoms
on rain-black trees. The enormous eyes of horses. Rock-weed, slate.
The world loving us, who probably have never loved enough,
never dared let ourselves go that far into its beauty.

From

Late Psalm

2004

AT THE PUBLIC MARKET

(i)

Abandon all hope, reads the hand-scrawled sign
propped beside the lobster tank—some joker
brooding on its murky doom, which looks

more like the world unformed and void,
stirred by a mind feeling that sluggish urge
to make itself known, a mind struggling

into form, water to gel, to claw and tail,
oozing its way out of slime, stumbling
among bottom feeders, grovelers, creeps

all bunched up, feelers adither
over their future's watery inferno.
How innocent Dante seems at first—

trembling and clutching at Virgil his guide,
as if he hadn't constructed that bucket
of dry ice himself, and personally

tossed each specimen in. Such a din
of marketing all around, it's easy
to be wilted by guilt, or to rage at

whoever made this place. But to watch
how lobsters madly scramble, you have to
bend close, look through your own shadow

into the tank's dim algae light,
where a few black beads fiercely eye back—
grabbers and pinchers clawing their way

to the top of some little heap.
And for what? I suddenly have to ask,
trembling, here, in the middle of my life.

(ii)

The flesh of swordfish swirls like wood grain
around a knot, and the tuna's a dark rose,
its petals packed tight beside the bright
fine-grooved salmon making raw seem sweet:

such a beautiful display of how we eat
and are eaten. The crabs, oysters, mussels,
big and bigger shrimp in their gray shrink-wrap—
imagine not being able to eat,

having to repeat the rounds of these stalls
stunned like the gluttons on Terrace Six, who look
but can't touch as hunger crawls through muscle
and mind. Imagine the millionth time passing

bins piled with scallops like the jellied whites
of eyes collected by a mad despot.
And bass on ice, tiered rows of snapper,
gold racing stripes lined up with such care

each bright red unblinking bull's-eye is clear—
a good kind of grief Dante manages to say,
reading on each passing face shrunk down
to skull the word *Omo* (man), as if life

is a hunger we shouldn't rush to quell,
as if we shouldn't even want to dull
our appetite's relentless drive
till it arrives at what can't be consumed.

(iii)

Pineapples all patchwork and spikes,
with green rooster crowns; pomegranates
catacombed, and in each small waxy room

an edible jewel; barrels
of lumpen potatoes, country onions
and their city cousins, the lilies,

decked out in fancy names like handles
to grasp when the petals are gone: *Adelina,*
Latoya, Louvre, Solomio . . .

And tiny peppers with no earthly use
but to be viewed; coffee beans burlapped
and brought from Kenya, Zimbabwe, Peru;

wheels and wedges of cheese, balls and bricks,
made with mold, the whey whipped out,
so the curds can curdle, be coated

with linen, bark, grape leaves, or wax, then left
to sit and age like old folks in rockers—
we eat what time does to earth, fragrant

or foul. Even when Dante gets to heaven
and there's no more plot, just shadowless light,
saints content with their allotted flames,

even there, he meets a widow with more lovers
than she can name, blazing among the rest,
happily spared for her generous heart.

And maybe our best chance, yet, is to believe
the world's not empty, not *nothing* in fine clothes,
but *everything,* marrow, muscle, skin.

QUEEN OF THE NIGHT

For Ruth Welting

They're not gone yet, those notes she lifts
from deep inside, like a quarterback
she says, lofting up and out, not knowing
if they'll be caught or spin down off orbit
and slip from the receiver's hands. Last week
they soared across the opera's stadium

so everyone received the pass. *Brava! Brava!*–
five full minutes before they let her go.
Next day, she walked up to the gate, got bumped
flight after flight, as if from elation, she says—
as if it's a law: one day the Met, the next
you can't get out of bed. There's the time she rose

from the basement on a tiny platform—
no rails, stagehands had to stuff her skirts—
but something snagged on the wobbly ascent
into smoke and lights, so just as her aria
climbed to its heights her skirts came undone.
Comic version, same rule: whatever rises, falls.

Sometimes, though, it seems to go another way:
that voice arriving uninvited to both her sister
and herself, lifting them out of such a lowdown
childhood, for years those bad times still bubbled
and steamed underneath any stage they were on,
like the opera's cave of death, its dry ice

and writhing souls backlit on a gauzy veil.
Once she blew that voice off in smoke rings and slurs,
didn't ask for it back, though it came, deepened
into parts she'd been too high for: the Queen's
daughter, who pleads to her lover's back—
pure *sehnsucht*, "longing beyond longing,"

———

the part her sister sang, whose own stupendous voice
was choked off in a husband's seething rage—
no one there to hear the last cries crushed
in her throat. *Sehnsucht.* Over tea,
she closes her eyes, and that aria wells up
then trails off to such thin decibels,

such quiet notes they could sift through loam
and stir the dead—if longing didn't dissolve
before it got to bone, if motion didn't
involve both rise and fall, sack and Hail Mary,
the Met's bright cheers, then next morning's lone soul
at the gate, ordinary voice seeking flight.

ELEGY WITH TRAINS

For Shirley Roses

My friend would tell the story of those two men
who don't know where the train is going,
so after it stops at a depot in that sham
of a real journey, they run to climb back on
the boxcars gathering speed, heading

for Bergen-Belsen. Hard to talk after that.
Though once pushing strollers we respun the facts,
made vodka-numbed Nazis chuckle *lucky*
bastards and shrug as the engine chugs on,
so the two dapper young men race

then gasp, slumping down on the tracks
at the start of their spared lives. That's where
it always broke down, my friend's head full
of ghetto stats, the true story of trains—
Spared? I can still see her stop and glare,

You call that spared? Across different cities
and twenty years our conversation ran: *Scratch*
a gentile deep enough and you get a Nazi . . .
Who can say they wouldn't collaborate . . .
Then this turned up in her parents' safe

deposit box: a photo marked *Poland—*
grandparents she thought had died in a trench
they dug themselves at bayonet point,
but here they are grinning while sunlight
beams on a sleek, finned sedan—hidden

all these years, as if it had been heresy
to her folks that someone survived, happy
to drive away from those trains in such
a big fishy car—her folks, who lived through
the war in Brooklyn, as if in shame,

vowing never to find life sweet again,
never to wait underground without
staring down the track's long perspective
into that vanishing point of bitter graves.
I was suicidal, my friend said,

until I got cancer. We were walking
a steep hill, ice cream cones in our hands,
stopping every few yards to rest,
her unshaded eyes staring at rose vines,
jet trails, late sun on brick, drinking them in.

That was the last time we met, so I don't
have to picture her dying on the year's
longest night, struggling for breath, alone
in her apartment, only those grandparents
framed beside her: my friend, whose silver loops

now hang from my ears, whose two earnest men
won't stop racing after that train. I don't
have to picture it slowing down, or the look—
we could never decide on the look—
in the guards' eyes, when they put out their hands.

PHOTOGRAPHER

August Sander, 1876–1964

Notary, Butcher, Repossessor:
  his ambition—to collect them all,
    to catalogue the age. But *Writer,*
Varnisher, Village Band—the types divide,
  individuate. So, he takes more:
    City Children, warily eyeing him,
Widower with Sons, slumped in grief.
  He believes we can see things as they are,
    the whole flux, "favorable to us or not."
Then a wind blows through the streets of Cologne,
  across the clothesline strung on his roof,
    knocking a print loose, the photograph
fluttering down into a citizen's hand,
  confiscator's fist. "This isn't truth,"
    the Nazis sneer—*Transvestites* on pages
facing *Aryan Youth,* so when the book's closed
  they kiss. Still, he insists: *Cretin, Tramps,*
    Dwarves—things as they are, not the myth.
After wind, come secret police, bombs.
  Then war's end, and fire set by looters
    finally burns the plates he's buried,
as if an age could categorically refuse
  to let itself be known, disdaining
    our glance: like these two *Bohemians,*
so fixed on each other they seem to say
  we can't possibly know what they see,
    or this *Unemployed* man, hat in hand
on the empty street, head shaved—
  has his hair been sold, spent?
    Or these: *Circus People,* lounging
beside their caravan, clustered around
  an old Victrola—record on, needle down—
    who stare as if they're trying to hear
how the tinny song thins as it passes
  through the lowered gaze of a woman
    leaning at the door, as it grazes

the black man's braided suit, presses
against his wary eye, fixed—now
that no one else is left—on us.

BACK WITH THE QUAKERS

You think you can handle these things:
sunlight glinting off a red Jaguar
honking at the old woman who has snagged

her shopping cart on a snow rut,
or the swaggering three-piece suit who steps
outside the bank, earless to the mossy voice

at his feet asking for spare change,
but then the crunch of something, nothing really,
under your shoe—a dirty comb, a pen cap—

completely undoes you, and it's too much,
too much, being balanced, considering
the complexity of all sides in one

syntactically correct sentence.
All the driver has to say is, "Move it,
Lady," and you're back with the Quakers

who trained you to lie still and limp in the street.
Three days they stepped on your hair,
ground cigarettes a half inch from your nose,

while you lay there, trying to be against
violence, your fists tight as grenades
and a payload of curses between your teeth,

O woman, with a mind Picasso
could have painted, giving you many cheeks,
each one turned a different way.

ALL QUESTIONS TO BE ANSWERED, NO

I thought of snow, but it was still summer.
    I pictured my friend doing the mashed potato
        to James Brown in her living room, but she
was in bed wincing when she turned, bald,
    testy with death. Is laughter gone forever?
        Sometimes I just like saying it: *No.*
Will we ever stop longing to feel
    feathers spread out from our arms, a tail
        at our waists, little twiggy feet—and blue,
can we please be blue? Can we give up
    words and just scat, eat, fuss a little,
        soar and sleep? Lord of the scabrous,
Lord of street theater and widowers,
    of the timorous and blustering, are we
        allowed to be tired, to pull down the shades,
to feel grateful for who we are—not like
    the pudgy child in the supermarket
        fingering cookies, the skinny mother
who yanked him away, then flicked me off
    with her eyes? Lord of my friend reading
        mysteries all night when the pain wakes her,
Lord of women who do amazing things
    with hair: huge fountains, wedding cakes of hair—
        I see their clients every Friday on the bus.
Lord of the bus, of the standing and seated,
    the tax collector longing to weep
        in his rented car—will we ever be done
with grieving, with little boys singing
    to their lunch boxes, brittle mothers
        with chemical hair? Sweet Lord of hair,
beaded curtains and narrow fringes—the girl
    on the bus telling her friend, "I know a kid
        grows marijuana in his hair"—thick falls
and little sprouts, conks, tonsures, wigs
    the wind can't dishevel, and underneath,
        underneath—will we ever be done?

VERTICAL MELANCHOLY

Poor moth-eaten lawn, weedy and pissed on,
poor maple trees, dry and brittle in June.
I came out to read de Andrade
tell himself *Carlos, keep calm, love is what
you're seeing now* . . . And maybe I dozed,

that's why in just four stanzas the sky's grown
heavy as rumpled bed sheets. Now a creak,
casket-like, from a scary movie,
or a sign swinging on one rusty hinge
in a storm. Birds content with bare branch

markings on their backs. That creak again—*saints
crossing themselves, vertical, melancholy?*
Or just these two slender trunks rubbing
each other? Desperate, undomesticated
tree-love, here in my parched yard

where the clothesline has squealed on its pulleys
all spring, and my friend will never again sit,
asking, "Why don't you throw out that wreath?"
still hanging on the fence, hardly more brown
than the leaves—color of choking, her voice

trying to clear itself, that shallow cough.
And her husband can do nothing now,
her teenage daughter can't find a book
long enough, deep enough to hide in.
And now the first raindrops magnify the words:

*Love in the dark, no, love in the daylight,
is always sad.* Because the last hinge
wears thin, words blur, puckered by rain.
What are words, anyway? Let rain
with its pure invisible ink write this

letter to the trees, to the men and women
in their motels, lying in one another's arms—
today a kiss, tomorrow no kiss . . . Let rain
fall on the person writing these words
who for once doesn't care what she'll do

with the heavy weight of afternoon
falling like flowers dropped on her friend.
It's useless to resist . . . Let rain ask all the bereft:
Could even this be love, love in the dark,
no, in the daylight, what is pouring now?

SHORE WALK WITH MONK

Whoever lived here is gone, but a slick
staircase remains in the broken shell,
damaged just enough to suggest secret
recesses spiraled inside where *something*
slid down to poke out its head,

and when a threat appeared, scurried
or oozed back along those pearly halls.
Someone stood catatonic when shaken down
by cops, but when he felt safe on the bandstand
he'd step out and dance, flap his elbows

like nubby wings, then back to the keyboard
to pick up his place, foot kicking
the piano's invisible flywheel.
Those were the years everyone changed shape,
painters squinted, poked their heads outside the frame.

Why have frames at all—or canvas, or paint?
And why not play the least expected note
so the music's a double exposure,
what's there and what isn't superimposed,
a melodic house all fretwork and jut,

as if any minute the whole structure
might topple? But a house, once you've entered,
nothing four-square will do. You want those
crooked doors, those circular steps ending
in pure misterioso, you need

those rooms suspended over a bay
where sunlight keeps changing tempo and key—
or so I was thinking when my tape started
to chirp like a hip calliope,
and I took it out to see if I could rewind,

finger holding one reel, pencil turning
the other, like one of his visitors
fidgeting while Monk sits wordless for hours
or grinds his teeth. Funny, how he gets me out
of my own head's maze, its slippery hall of mirrors,

when he could go so far inside his own,
nothing moved but his eyes. Or he'd spend days
in constant motion, pacing and spinning
till the turbulence inside finally found
a room with a bed and laid itself down.

Weeks it could take to stumble back out—
which might explain all the doors and tilted
balconies in his musical house,
Magritte windows with their starry skies
painted on glass, while a perilous void

expanded inside. I'm off the beach,
beside my car by now, unraveling
a Mobius strip of Monk, Monk billowing
over dune grass and rocks, ringing the car's
antenna, Monk in hundreds of tiny

accordion pleats I couldn't undo
no matter how I try, all spiraling out
of their plastic shell, catching the light, pouring
a kind of broken music the maker's
done with, just slipped out of and left behind.

AFTER THAT

In Lakewood, New Jersey, they'd rock all day
on the porch of the old Jewish hotel—women
sputtering like those newsreels of Europe,
where they must have trudged through snow
in battered boots with newspaper socks,
looking for streets that no longer existed.

Back and forth they'd rock, muttering like pigeons,
old women who rolled their stockings just
to the knees as if that was dressing enough.
And they'd huff themselves out of their chairs
as if rising even a little was more than too much.
All through childhood's eyeglasses and cavities,

through first pumps with skinny five-inch heels
and pointy toes, I couldn't walk fast enough
past that chorus of mourners lined up,
davening in wicker chairs, unstoppable clocks,
cradles endlessly rocking the world's woes,
dividing who saw from who shut their blue eyes.

I thought they only stopped the heavy creak
of their grief when I walked past. New shoes
dyed to match a prom gown, new lipstick, blush—
I'd swear they looked and scoffed. But maybe
they didn't notice me at all. Maybe
they were just grinding the past down

to one coarse meal of bone. Still, I can't
enter a store without hearing their voices—
so much vinegar even God would shudder,
would rummage through bins, wanting
to give them something, anything at all,
those fierce widows rocking forever

on the guest house porch, refusing to enter,
refusing to leave, having outlasted whole cities.
What would you ask for after that—
Some bright pleasure, a new truth?
Loden green pumps with stiletto heels?
That the world end, that the world continue?

BASS LINE

For Milt Hinton

He needs a bigger body, bull fiddle
to make that thump, that deeper pulse, he needs

four fat inflexible strings made of gut
wrapped by steel, so he can pluck each night

that tree and its strange fruit, its slumped shoulders
and bulging eyes. . . . As he fingers the neck,

as he frets, keeps the time, he can take
those naked feet hung like weights on a stopped clock.

If it's too much to say one sight winds up
a life and keeps it running, still

some things are burned into the eyes
like a maker's mark seared into walnut

belly or back, history always there,
no matter how the body is patched

and reglued, the gut and steel fine-tuned.
It's a deep groove in the brain,

whether you play on top or behind the beat,
walk the line or break out: to know a man

can be waiting for a train and because the crowd's
riled up get taken. If death unmakes him,

maybe music's a way of weeping,
of cradling the broken body,

its strained neck, its eyes that tried to jump
at what they saw, and sad hands, sad hands

that couldn't lift to brush a fly.
Night after night, rhythm wants to unwind

the wire cable from that tree, sway
the mob away from its drunken rush.

So if he humps that stiff body night
after night, if he slaps and slaps? It's to

accent the offbeat, strengthen the weak, swing
like somebody who knows what swinging is.

TO WALT WHITMAN IN HEAVEN

Things that look good and aren't: high fashion,
Manifest Destiny, limp wires the electrician thinks
are dead till he grabs hold and then, oh Infinite-
coursing-through-finite—thank God his spastic dance

is only a shock—one yelp and he shakes
it off. Not so easy for the girl next door
feeling her first kiss begin to fester
as the young man's buddies drive by hooting

and one calls out, *How far did ya get? Whadda
we owe?* It's enough to make everything
look bad. So, a list then of what turns out
to be good: the loud-mouthed parrot

down the block that scared off two robbers,
the junior prom I spent alone in my room
reading you, Walt Whitman, your great
barbaric yawp entering my mind like salt

water coursing through fresh, stinging my wounds,
till every image was sharp—the lunatic,
the lily-faced boy in the makeshift hospital,
contralto, runaway, cloud scud, your voice

whispering through sea spray to ferry crowds,
just as you feel, so I felt. . . . What doesn't change
and remain, remain and grow strange? The lace
bodice from my mother's slip my daughter

now sews onto the cuffs of her new jeans,
the crooked front tooth that has traveled through
how many kisses from my mother's mouth
to mine, and on to my son. What is a list?

The neighbor girl goes through her catalog
of moves under the hoop—sky hooks, layups,
fall-away jumpers. Long after dark, she's out there
dribbling her heart on the asphalt, tossing it up,

nothing but net. Painful, yes, but how else
will she get to that sweet agony within,
your great loitering contradictions? She dodges
and spins, as if shedding a skin, steps around

the driveway to keep the motion light flaring
as she passes from shadow into Technicolor,
banks a shot, jabs the air to cheer herself on,
point guard, center and crowd all in one,

and I almost see you in the dark,
on the fringe, though I can hardly say what
you mean, in the sweet mysterious night vapor
hovering over blacktop and lamp-green lawn.

LATE PSALM

I am hating myself for the last time.
    I'm rolling up angst like a slice of bread,
squishing it into a glob that will rot
    into blue medicine—another joke,
delivered by God, who when you finally
    elbow and nudge to the front of the line,
says, *Oh, but the first shall be last* . . .
    I'm considering the roadside grass,
all dressed up and headed straight for the fire.
    "Who isn't?" say the flames,
though it's easy to pretend not to hear
    in this mountain resort with its windows
all finely dressed for the busiest season
    filled with glass fish, turquoise earrings,
infusers that turn weeds into tea.
    "Who isn't poor already?" sing the stalks
of dried milkweed, though it's hard to
    imagine these shoppers in bright ski jackets
coated with road grit, dust from the chunks
    of bituminous coal left outside mines
for the poor to glean. The poor—
    just driving by those bent figures,
filling their plastic bags, here in the 1990s,
    made me stop nodding *yeah yeah*
to the music and pull off the road,
    stunned by the way the years press hard
to fossilize plants, and the poor too,
    who seem to age a month for every
middle-class day. How could they
    possibly hear a blade of grass sigh, "Poor?
There is no such thing." Did I say
    I'm hating myself for the last time?
It's not easy, but I'm loving instead—
    brown teeth, Kool Aid mustaches, swollen
knuckles, nature's answer to all questions—
    prodigality, those countless insects

and missionary weeds spending themselves
     freely and as far as I can tell, never
rescinding a thing. I'm loving a man
     with his pockets full of pen caps, receipts,
crumpled dollars to put in a beggar's
     dented cup, briefcase bulging with papers,
leftover crusts for the ducks,
     and out of his eyes little fish of light,
glimmering minnows and fingerlings
     leaping between us, flashing
like the tiny carp we watched last night
     in the restaurant tank, appearing through
weeds, miniature castles, a bubbly
     tube resuscitating their atmosphere.
Do they ever conceive of worlds outside
     the only one they've known? Because *he* is,
my man says they're serene, swimming in
     a seamless rippling universe,
not quaking at the sight of monstrous eyes
     leering into the tank, not aching
with the lure of light, lethal burn of air,
     declaring their world a glass prison house.
Rich or poor—who decides? Who wrote
     the stories in which women cry out
all the more when folks tell them to hush,
     and beggars asking for money
get wild rapture instead?

BECAUSE WE IMAGINE
A JOURNEY

and don't know how difficult the passage,
we leave gifts to help the dead cross over:
my teacher's black beret tucked in her coffin,

my nephew's notebooks, in case he needs
to recall how long he resisted the demons.
And for the small child freshly buried,

each time I walk the dog there's something new—
another pinwheel, a stuffed rabbit,
ceramic angel, photo of her mother

wrapped in plastic and tape,
as if someone whispered, *Fly, little soul,
back here, and hover.* All summer

that someone was pleading,
the way I see now I must have been,
in September, making the minister open

cupboards and desks for something to hold
a few granules of my mother.
But when he poured the rest of her out

in the churchyard, under a cross made of shrubs,
with the family gathered, it seemed wrong
to hold anything back from the journey,

even a part so small it fit
in a brown plastic medicine bottle.
No wonder the bagpiper practices here

his eerie songs—so unearthly they could be
wails made by souls force-marched off,
and loath to go, bunched up

like crowds at a border, great ghostly hordes
that pick up the song when the piper stops,
gusts driving a throng of leaves skittering

up the steep road. Such a huge wind
it surges through trees, bends them nearly in two,
and as if to linger in the tumult longer

an elderly couple walks backward
uphill, hand-in-hand, as I head down
pulled by my dog who stops to sniff the air,

then shakes his tags, lunging happily
toward the cattails and feathered water
of the pond. Watching ducks skid in,

materializing from all directions,
raucous and comic, around a man's
magnetic bag of crumbs, I can't help thinking

it's possible there is no death after all,
just a thin veil between one life and another,
lifting sometimes in a wail, or wind, an eddy

of leaves wrapping itself around the legs
of a grieving mother, or telling a child
it's all right, all right now, to let go.

LAST BOAT

We were waiting for the ferry,
lolling on the lowest ramp, on floats,
shifty with wave slush, dip and sway.

We were sun-seared, sapped, soaking in
the latticework, wooden scaffolding,
stacks of lobster traps, pilings stained black

from creosote and tar, green with seaweed
combed out on receding waves, swirled back
by water's slap and curl: levels and lengths

of working docks, creaky planks, crossbars
of tacked asbestos for stopping the slip
on slick days—the whole wet rush,

the gleaming run-down fertile place.
We were sitting on a dock of the bay,
watching how matter melts into

quivery silks of light, a brilliant seethe,
a glittery tease of *there*
and *not there*, such dazzling manna.

We were squinting through shadows
at little flamelike fish flickering
among weeds—a whole world it seemed

flaring under the ramshackle,
barnacled, rock-bottom dock, all flow
and flown, and we were resting in

the brevity, the breve, breviary,
the never-ending not-me: waiting
for the ferry, wishing it wouldn't come.

From

Rough Cradle

2009

THE SEA ITSELF

Here, on solid ground, a blue jay lands,
beautiful and shrill, looking right at me,
banging a seed over and over, as if

he'll never get it right—another creature
I once crudely dismissed. I'm sorry
for all my old arrogant thoughts,

for the man who followed me
one whole summer, a grabber, swallower,
a devil in Bermuda shorts. But really,

his hands were so thin and shaky,
it was easy to slip through,
all it cost me was an old blouse,

the buttons flying off into the pine needles
and white sand of our struggle.
I left him on his knees weeping,

my blue shirt dripping from his hands.
Of course, I said *No*. But I'm sorry
I said it so fiercely that day

there wasn't room for pity or anything else.
I'm not sorry I said *No* to the storm tide
that dragged me out, then tossed me back

like an undersized fish, an hysterical teenager
flung on shore. Thick quilted clouds overhead,
sand blowing through tufts of beach grass—

such a total *No*, it became a kind of *Yes*,
so the world was suddenly everything at once,
solid and shifty, stormy and calm.

For years I told this story all wrong.
Even now, my words are just a net
holding fish, while the sea itself slides through,

that slippery, unfathomable
Yes & No, that everything-at-once
impossible to name—

even if you were spared,
even if you have many more songs
than the harsh one you learned so well.

DOING TIME

Prison poetry workshop

They call me "Babe" and make a kissing noise
from inside their bars and inside their rage.
Most of them are men, though they act like boys

who've played too hard and broken all their toys.
Now they're trying to break their metal cage.
They yell out "Babe," make that loud kissing noise

as if their catcalls mean they have a voice
routines and bells can't break. "It's just a phase,"
their parents must have said when they were boys.

Don't ask what they're in for; let them enjoy
their small audience, their short time on stage:
"Hey, Babe, how about—" then that kissing noise.

In class they want to rhyme, their way to destroy
all evidence of anguish on the page.
They can't bear to remember being boys.

Some study law, some use another ploy,
daydreaming they'll do time, but never age.
"Hey, Babe" means "kiss off" to that cellblock noise,
to broken men in here since they were boys.

CHILDHOOD

In my aquarium the fish went round
and round—kissing fish and clown fish
and one very blue fish with a mouth grimmer
than Grandfather, whom we could offend
without knowing. Then no amount of running
next door to beg through the locked screen,
What did I do? would help. No amount of
saying *sorry*, stammering on the first
snakelike S sizzling into frayed rope.

No amount of whistling to our dog Ruff
would make him stay and not race across fields
as if running were breathing to him.
But we wanted to fondle and smooch,
to throw sticks for him to fetch right back.
We chained him up because we loved him.
Grandfather must have felt this way about
whatever was inside his head he never let out,
his long list of reasons to be bitter,

that gene he fattened and passed on
to three generations, which probably was
passed on to him, locked midway in the chain,
since his own father caught an infection
from a horse and died just days after
conceiving him. Plant matter to coal, coal
to diamond—things pressed down long enough
turn hard, then somebody finds them precious
and snarls or hisses when you get close.

I really thought if I stood outside and stared
till I saw the exact moment the streetlight
came on, my dog would speak, my fish would
let me hold his golden fin-flutter to my lips,
and my own dead father would step out from
the vanishing point at the end of our street.
It was winter, so what I got was frostbite
and a weeping mother bathing my hands
in pans of cool water. But what if

----

we could reel through our memories
to the exact moment before the salt
went into the wound, that moment of pure
perception before the hardening began?
Leaning from her arms to hand an apple
to a horse's brown teeth and velvet nose,
laughing at its warm breath—"Little Miracle"
my grandfather was then, child number ten,
birthed out of his mother's long black clothes.

ELEPHANT SEALS

Muffled thunder like clouds rolling over
in sleep, and mirrored underneath—
such gray sodden bodies, enormous slugs

with Spandexed buttocks and thighs.
One, with his long dangling nose
like something lunar, tumorous, lumbers

across the sand, nudging through others who arf,
who rise on fins, then belly-flop down.
Easy to argue from nature anything

at all—dead end in evolution's maze,
or evidence of God's wild earthy wit.
But the bulls argue over their harems,

one youth galumphing toward a battle-scarred
alpha who rears and roars, till the upstart
backs off, biding his time. Around them

the sea sputters, rain pocks the sand, the pod
piles up. If this is the utterly other,
still, when one drowsy-eyed mother,

lolling as her baby nuzzles in to nurse,
lifts a fringed, finger-like fin to scratch,
everyone watching feels an itch.

LULLABY IN BLUE

The child takes her first journey
through the inner blue world of her mother's body,
    blue veins, blue eyes, frail petal lids.

Beyond that unborn brackish world so deep
it will be felt forever as longing, a dream
    of blue notes plucked from memory's guitar,

the wind blows indigo shadows under streetlights,
clouds crowd the moon and bear down on the limbs
    of a blue spruce. The child's head appears,

midnight pond, weedy and glistening,
draws back, reluctant to leave that first home.
    Blue catch in the mother's throat,

ferocious bruise of a growl, and out slides
the iridescent body—fish-slippery
    in her father's hands, plucked from water

into such thin densities of air,
her arms and tiny hands stutter and flail,
    till he places her on her mother's body,

then cuts the smoky cord, releasing her
into this world, its cold harbor below
    where a blue caul of shrink-wrap covers

each boat gestating on the winter shore.
Child, the world comes in twos, above and below,
    visible and unseen. Inside your mother's croon

there's the hum of an old man tapping his foot
on a porch floor, his instrument made from one
    string nailed to a wall, as if anything

can be turned into song, always what is
and what is longed for. Against the window
    the electric blue of cop lights signals

somebody's bad news, and a lone man walks
through the street, his guitar sealed in dark plush.
        Child, from this world now you will draw your breath

        and let out your moth flutter of blue sighs.
Now your mother will listen for each one,
        alert enough to hear snow starting to flake

        from the sky, bay water beginning to freeze.
Sleep now, little shadow, as your first world
        still flickers across your face, that other side

        where all was given and nothing desired.
Soon enough you'll want milk, want faces, hands,
        heartbeats and voices singing in your ear.

        Soon the world will amaze you, and you
will give back its bird-warble, its dove call,
        singing that blue note which deepens the song,

        that longing for what no one can recall,
your small night cry roused from the wholeness
        you carry into this broken world.

A SONG IN THERE

To stave off trouble, the old bluesmen are singing,
without a doubt, singing—on doorsteps, in bare yards
with folding chairs tipsy on tree roots. No tape rolling,
no old rattling film, no spotlight, gold tooth, big car.

Forgive me, my heroes, for thinking this tragic,
that a front porch with crickets and night fog
isn't enough, a dusty juke joint with straw-strewn floor
buoyant under sore but dancing feet.

I want to believe that even books burned to ash
were worth the long nights of their making, that a song
drifting on invisible waves still exists somewhere
however faint, washing an unknown shore.

You who were not recorded to be touched up
and played back later, did you love the raw world more,
love the shy songbird's refusal to be seen?
My mentors, you who heard a minor chord,

a blue note struck two fields away, and ambled over
to swell the sound, joining the blue breakup, breakdown,
the song talking back to the battered life—forgive me
for even once wanting to sit in the sleek car

airbrushing through town. In its wake the world
resumes, briar and dust, heartbeat and sky, nest
squalling with hunger. And there, broke or flush,
blind or sighted, you sang. Traveling by hay wagon,

boxcar, jalopy, fingers like knotted sticks, a thicket
in your voice, on unpaved corners for spare change,
you sang. Over you the clouds would bundle and shred,
the night send out sparks. Then earth closed over.

Now the air's full of echo and remix.
Still, in my mind's graveyard, I am laying flowers
at your unmarked feet, fingering the Braille
of a tree's lichened trunk, all splotch and ridge—

your monument, bearing wounds where limbs were
cut off. I know the music's in there, somewhere
rising, leaf thirst and bent note, a song in there,
root-crooned, wind-strummed and rising.

GRAVITY AND GRACE

*Grace fills empty spaces, but it can only enter where
there is a void to receive it.*
—SIMONE WEIL

Simone Weil, it's hard to concentrate on you
with those three boys on the next bench
blowing up balloons and letting them go,
all squirt and grunt, fizzling into—

the void, you'd probably say. And leaving
a void too—if spent breath becomes exhaust,
if everything we do ends up empty.
So, prayer becomes a little death

as we pour our desires into words
that fill to bursting, then leave our lips
to corkscrew and sputter, spitting out air,
selfless, anonymous enough to rise.

Now the boys race up the slide, all high-fives
and laughter, blowing off gravity, while I read
you'd like to be blown away, see a landscape
as it is when I am not there—as if the self

blocks God the way bodies block light.
Thus your executor was to destroy
all record of your mind—those notebooks filled
with stark meditations as Hitler railed,

as death camps filled and ghettos burned. *Love is
not consolation,* you wrote, *it is light,*
meaning that fierce headlamp of attention
which leaves the self in shadow and trains

its high beam on the void where prisoners
huddle under gravity's dark weight,
and grace, if it comes, comes in secret,
to those struck dumb, trembling in the glare.

125

THE DRINKING GOURD

For homework we were to connect the stars
into constellations along dotted lines,
but when I stepped outside, those lines tore
apart like perforations, and the stars
scattered. Chicken feed tossed in a dark yard,
water flung from a bucket.

Underneath that crazy fizz of light
I was illiterate, able to read
just one shape, the dipper, what fugitive
slaves called "the drinking gourd" in the song
our teacher sang about the North Star
leading them through dense woods and bogs.

When the evening news showed mothers
shrieking at little kids trying to walk
to school, or big kids getting yanked
off their soda fountain stools,
I'd step outside. No color on our old
black-and-white, just grownups snarling.

Away from the slant of window light,
under the sky's bright litter, I'd look
for that drinking gourd, and shiver.
Twig snap, dried vines, night things
grabbing from behind. Then something new—
raging faces, ready to tear apart

the children walking slowly, their eyes fixed
on the door straight ahead, while around them,
barely held by sawhorses and police,
those mothers gone feral bared their teeth
and screamed as if the stars had come undone
and were spiraling out of the sky.

TERESKA

After the photo by David Seymour,
"TERESKA, A CHILD IN A RESIDENCE FOR DISTURBED
CHILDREN," *Poland, 1948*

She's been given chalk and asked to draw
a picture of home, so it's hard to see
in her spiraled lines an abstract design,
hard to think "antic delight in pure form,"
when she stands beside the board, looking
fixed and wary, having just mapped a world
slashed with barbed wire, a world crossed out,
going up in chalky flames, yellow smoke
scribbling its dust over roofs, curtains,
books and dolls, whatever a house once held.
Someone's put a ribbon in her hair,
but she's hardly a little girl, glaring
as if to warn: ask for something pretty,
and she'll cat-scratch with that chalk,
claw and hiss—this *is* her home now,
this world found only by tearing up the map,
this town without streets, house with no mother,
no music, no lights, just a heap of rubble
where a mind lives hunched down and feral,
defending the one thing it knows.

BEGONIA

Each evening I believe in the everlasting, and fear
by dawn blight will have crept into the garden.

But each morning there you are, watery blossoms
dripping from the lip of multiple green faucets,

a magician's trick of scarf after soft yellow
and orange scarf rippling from a sleeve.

How to name your layers of petalwork,
your shades of peach, apricot, lemon, goldfinch—

labia it's all right to look at? Again
and again your bright orange pods burst

into a bush full of canaries, each one singing.
Still, I can't forget that tyrants tend gardens,

Stalin ordered executions among bright buds
which continued to unfurl. Such fragrant treachery.

Or were they earth's efforts to dissuade?
Clearly, you have no ill will,

so if there's a judgment, and a witness is needed
to testify against us, let it be you,

before whom the only penance is awe.
O delicate teacups with so many rims

drinking's unthinkable—
O galaxy of florescent stars fluttering down

on the just and the unjust, long into September.

WHAT THE WORLD WANTS

On this northern rim of the world,
the cold seeps through worn collars
like the ocean's iciest breath, like death,

or the whole second shift, spilling out
of the plant into night's deep freeze,
unscarfed throats bait for the wind's teeth.

At week's end I take my thin paycheck
into an overpriced shop and linger
under the saleswoman's chilly glare,

fingering soft weaves I can't afford,
dangling fringe in my palm, weighing rent
against cashmere, cable against chenille.

In the three-way mirror I line up to eye
my triplicate selves: one face oozes
with desire, one scowls, furrowed up,

feeling duped by vanity's profiteers,
the middle one sighs and turns away,
baring her chapped throat to the world.

But inside my patched jacket and scuffed boots,
that self stands on the twilit street
and can't help seeing the sky turn pale silk,

its mist like rain tamed and spun into fringe.
She'll stomp to shake it off, mutter about deceit's
flimsy gauze draped over necessity.

And yet, under the sky's late glow, its dark
translucent blue nothing can duplicate,
she has to think maybe the world wants

a little shimmer and gloss, wants its workers
when the bottle's empty, the table bare,
to notice the cloth's lavish folds.

LIFE AND HOLINESS

I couldn't finish the book because the end
no longer existed, the final words on *life*
and *holiness*, that old coin with its two sides
impossible to see at once, so each face
makes you long for the other—unless, of course,
the coin's been rubbed down, almost out,
as my book was, not dog-*eared*, but dog *chewed*,
its upper corners gnawed to raggedy pulp,
a big chunk torn off its lower right,
and the whole book ending coverless
on page 118, so it's hard to read
the thoughts without thinking of their fate,
the message bound to what carries it:
Life and Holiness by Thomas Merton
bound to our dog named Dreug, Russian for *friend,*
who also ate the edge of my purple dress
as I sat talking on the couch, plus a wooden apple,
and every chair rung in the house. It's hard
not to think of the monk being chewed on
by silence, gnawed down, past ritual and custom,
to a desert of naked prayer, a dark night
where nothing's left of the self's empty shell,
the soul cracked open for something else to rush in,
which the words were just getting to
when Dreug, that zealous friend, aching and driven,
turned the matter into slobber and wag,
his new teeth editing, so the book
ends with:

> ... For such ...
> ... lovers of God, all things, whether they appear ...
> ... actuality good. All things manifest the ...
> ... All things enable them to grow in ...

Here it stops, the promise digested,
our big brown dog a better reader than I,
licking his lips, swallowing the words, taking in
the *such* and *all things*, however they appear.

And was the back cover *good,* the spine glue,
the wood or rag pulp of each missing page? "Complete
and unabridged," it says just where the teeth marks
bite, where the paper's rough edge, its newly exposed
microscopic threads meet air and morning light,
as if words could turn into *life,* into window glass
with bickering sparrows, children walking
to school, as Dreug, with his spotted face,
his feathery toes, watches *all things*
manifest the—enable them to grow in—
As to *holiness,* you lovers of God, must all things
come to an edge where words stop, and hunger—
that faithful friend who eats away what once
would have been so easy to read—begins?

Otherwise Unseeable

2014

ALMS

Small as a fly bump, the little voice
behind me calling *Miss, Miss,* wanted
a dollar, maybe for food as she said

in that voice of mist, so plaintive
and soft it could have come from inside
my own head, a notch below whisper,
voice of pocket lint, frayed button hole,

voice of God going gnat small. I shivered
and stopped. I looked for the source,
and there it was again, *Miss,* so slight

it wobbled moth-like on air,
up from a bare trash-filled recess
beside the post office steps. Yes,
I gave the dollar. But I had seven

in my wallet, so clearly that voice
wasn't small enough, still someone
else's sorrow, easy to brush off,

till later that night, in bed, I heard it
again, smaller—*miss, miss,* little fly strafe
troubling sleep—not a name at all,
but a failure, a lack, a lost chance.

STILL LIFE WITH LIGHT BULB

How much energy spent on envy!
Burning all night, the light bulb knows

that an apple's still richer in the world's eye.
Though the bulb glows through fog

the way an apple doesn't—still, it's not
loved, not found at the world's start,

doesn't have its own alphabet page,
its own story of fall and attraction.

Can you read in the evening under an apple,
or turn it down low when your lover arrives?

An apple can't incubate eggs.
So, why are only apples polished on a shirt

and given to the teacher,
as if their dull inner stars could ever shine?

At least, the light bulb tells itself, nobody
draws an apple over the superhero's head

to show he's had a brilliant thought.
No, in fact, an apple's one idea

was very bad—just *eat, eat, eat me.*
And how dark the world became then.

THE WIND AND THE CLOCK

The wind dresses itself in trees, handbills,
dust balls, feathers and rags—anything to be seen—
unlike the upright clock in its polished box
sure of the world's respect for synchronized
numbers, the world's need for balance and weight.

Oh wait, the wind cries, shaking the window
in its sash, aching to get near the clock,
to knock at its door, unlatch the wooden world
inside. And once there? The clock knows
the wind would toss its weights like halyards

clanging in a stormy boatyard, hurl sand
in its fine-toothed gears, or lick its many
moon faces blank. The clock has seen how
wind strews autumn leaves like clothes tossed
on a lover's floor. Ah love, the wind sighs,

doesn't love always undo the very thing
done up to draw it in? But the clock thinks,
Faceless, what would I be, my hands spun
to a dizzy blur, my numbers scattered?
Numbers! the wind cries, does love keep

accounts? Doesn't Saint Peter say a day
and a thousand years are one and the same?
To want what you can't have is a fool's dream,
the clock tells the wind. To not take what
you want—*that* is love. And the wind,

which just now was stretching its invisible flag
in long rippling waves, falls limp.
So, its argument won, the clock strikes,
as if it had no second thoughts, never
once wished for wind's little ruckus

to swirl up old hair, dried wings, dust
from the stars, dust from the dead. The dead,
for whom all ticking has ceased, who come
to mind, and then go, invisible as the—
Oh, the wind, stirring its little eddies . . .

WILDFLOWERS

And it was commanded them that they should not hurt the
grass of the earth, neither any green thing . . .
—REVELATION 9:4

Consider the way they shudder in the aftermath
of coal trucks, farm trucks, the fast red car,

the way they sway in the backwind
of passing's vacuum, bending into the void,

the small rustle of what's left in the wake,
whatever is said on the edge of our leaving—

chicory, ironweed, aster, thistle, Joe-pye,
poorest of the poor—the way they stand

as if anonymous, knowing themselves
to be the blur passersby barely see,

the way they disappear when winter storms in,
and then come crowding back in spring,

the ground loving them the way it does not
love the golf course with its sleek chemical green—

coreopsis, milkweed, bittersweet, goldenrod,
sumac, wild carrot—

the way they bow to the passing waves
that release their seeds, needing only a little wind

to lift them across the field, a little rain,
a small crack in the hardpan to grow,

to possess the earth, as scripture says
they will, don't worry.

RAHSAAN

The sun sets off a whole lot of vibrations. . . . Sometimes on
the tenor I try to get a sun sound.
—RAHSAAN ROLAND KIRK

"You think I'm a clown?" He hits the switch
and the dressing room goes blind. Now who's
master of lights out, guide through the starless night?

Inside that vivid pitch, he hears flute-talk,
half goldfinch, half wheeze, hears a horn his dream
calls *moon zellar,* its banged-up metallic mouth.

Though sound has no weight, it needs a bell
and reed, needs muscle, breath, two puffed cheeks.
It can use a man with a bag full of horns,

willing to walk the rim between trickster
and sage, a man with the grit to keep going
if a stroke nails one hand down.

Certain sounds lie buried, heaped up, unheard,
till someone comes along with a cellar
behind his eyes, and inside that

a furnace blaze of dreams, a rush of notes
like coal shuttling into its metal house,
sound of flashlit siren-scan catching the gleam

of brash, a high C's shattered glass—
a man who says, "You want to hear sun vibes,
wind in B-flat? Well, shut your damn eyes."

THE ARGUMENT

September 1, 2009

On my way to the library,
sunlight on the first turning leaves,
goldenrod, coreopsis—and the crows
have something to say:

> *For the sake of the dead, for the sake*
> *of the murdered, don't wax too eloquent*
> *here under these dust-choked trees.*

Clear sky, seventy years since
Hitler invaded Poland, and we are here,
just one stray cloud for contrast.
But now a chorus of bleak thoughts,
a tree full of black fruit:

> *For the sake of the horses those Poles rode out*
> *against panzers and planes, for the sake of the spur wounds*
> *gouged in their sides, their buckling legs, for the men*
> *on their backs still human as they fell, and the other men*
> *inside their tanks turning into machines . . .*

Oh lighten up, I want to say. Morning glories
have scaled the stop sign, school buses are making
their first practice runs. The world goes on.
Still, the crows, those irascible grievers,
ratchet up their cries:

> *Goes on? Like bullhorns given over to endless*
> *yammering channels? Like this gasping hound*
> *the woman can barely contain on its leash, straining*
> *after a squirrel, a sunning cat, now you?—*

> *You, with your own black heart, carnivorous and wingless.*

Okay, okay. But can't I praise this late
summer day, the air rinsed clean?—and don't say,
Good for invasion. Let me have this brief walk
to return seven picture books showing children
a world of order and cheer, bears in ruffled aprons,
singing badgers—

and, I would like to point out, not one crow
tugging at roadkill guts, relishing the sound
of its own backfired voice.

But overhead, on a wire slung across the street,
that row of frayed umbrella wings—as if a clear sky's
no protection—and one rusty croak:

> *For the sake of the murdered, for the sake of the dead,*
> *for all that hasn't happened yet . . .*

WHAT'S LEFT OF HEAVEN

*I longed to put them down on my canvases, to get them
out of harm's way.*
—MARC CHAGALL

Not in a museum or book, but in sleep I saw
those paintings, little man in blue pants
afloat over the town, his violin,

playing the screech of crows flying up
after the first shot. Then many more rounds,
and a whole town rises—cow and bridge

and jumbled houses, wagons and goats
and red onion roofs flying apart. First
they fall down, hit hard, then rise back up

into the air, what's left of heaven. There is
a bride whose two feet don't quite touch earth,
a horse's eye—Oh Chagall, the past adrift,

cut up in wedges, the jagged glass become
blue windows into the *gone*, the *never*, the *once*,
held only by color and lead, longing and sleep.

Your tipsy villages crimson with flames,
where citizens pulled out toilets, church pews
and old sinks to stack up against panzers—

when I was young I thought that was *history*,
meaning *over and done*. Still, my dreams filled
with locked boxcars blurring the countryside

into streaks of color, the land through slats,
ghostly Bauhaus barracks with Prussian red
chimneys at the track's vanishing point,

as if sleep were insisting the *gone*
is not *over*, though the *once* will never return
to women wailing over their dead,

to men on crutches with sock-covered stumps,
and other men with eye patches over
the last thing they saw fly into their faces.

At night when the stars look like bright asters
blowing across the sky, I try not to think
of explosions, gas fires, burning trash,

of old wars whose winners carve up the world
into pieces that rub against each other
until sparks fly and flames erupt

that will scorch us all. Oh Chagall,
good to remind us of cows, hens, the moon
dangling from its rusty hinge, a fiddler

on his green violin, and the bride waiting
in midair for a man whose white shirt
blooms with dark roses. She drifts, silent,

moth-like over broken stalks, bearing no tools,
but a glass raised to the song that won't stop,
to the groom who hasn't yet come, to the world

that's still undone, its sparks and its young
who can't imagine that the light they see
comes from everything they love slowly burning.

RUSSIAN BELLS

*Soviet law made the ringing of bells illegal
in 1930*

Back then monks pulled the heavy ropes, toll
after toll, so the tongues formed tones, half-tones
from those tons of bronze, icons of sound,
the air thick with their clamorous rounds.

Insufferable God! What could Stalin do
but silence those voices, blow after blow,
beat them like kulaks? Each knell a dead Jew,
White Russian, Pole—he cut the ropes,

tore the belfries down, till, town after town,
straight to the tundra, the ground shuddered
where they crashed, the air gagged
as they were melted, remade into tanks

and guns, those sweet onions peeled down
to nothing, so the sky no longer stung.
What was left went untolled: pen scratch
across parchment, pistol crack blunted

by a bunker door. First the air recoiled,
then thinned, slipped between hinges,
spread in circles, seeking an ear, someone
to hear the body's thud, as one

after another was dragged off
to unmarked dirt, down where silence
blends with copper and tin, where almost
inaudible bones, heaps, half-bones wait

for earth to be unearthed, tongues loosened,
the ringing restored—in town after town,
that cloud-battering bronze, air unbound,
as the bells toll, they tell, each knell.

PRISONER BONHOEFFER

Executed April 9, 1945,
Flossenburg Concentration Camp

Better be wordless, he thinks, better Bach's swell
and diminuendo, *cantus firmus*, not quite drowned out

as notes rise and fall, until—is this it?—

the rising and falling are one, God in the midst,
not on some edge beyond, but *in*—

these cold cells, infested blankets, bitter voices.

Thus he writes to friends, "It is not by abstract argument,
but example . . . ," and "leave the insoluble unsolved. . . ."

So little can be spoken in letters,

so much not even hinted, certain hopes, one death
to prevent countless others . . .

Why mention headaches, bad teeth, cramped legs?

Better anthills, bees, the nest of titmice outside his window,
and thank you for the books, and here's a list of others.

And when the *Ethics* goes badly, there's verse—

rhyme to calm desire, temper the nightmares,
bear the new thought: release won't come,

God will not rise up out of war's insane machine

to pull him down from the wooden platform,
halt the order to strip and walk barefoot

———

up the scaffold steps,

where for him end and beginning are one
with the rope circling his neck

as time drops out from under, and is gone.

VANISHING ACT

Over the phone we're already bodiless,
though remember, Love, sound has a source,

and even a kiss made of mist
can touch a cheek and lodge in the mind.

Even a rose made of nothing but words.

It's not really a choice to be working on this
vanishing act. We hardly achieve form

before it starts going soft, opinions first,
then all those clamoring ambitions.

I can't help fretting about our next porous
existence, which one of us

will go first, last breath disappearing
in a crowd of molecules,

while the other is left alone
with a closet full of empty clothes.

Still, here on earth, it seems nothing
vanishes completely.

Fire leaves ash, a boat its wake wobbling
against the dock, and once we put our fingers

into the grooves where bullets gouged
the columns of the Dublin post office.

Remember the young gypsy girl who sat
on the curb, her breath already reeking

as she held out that squalling baby
and begged for spare change—

behind her how many curses, evictions,
burning wagons?

Until it's our turn, what do we really know?

Even despair, Kierkegaard said, is good—
enough to make a man

lift out of its withered case a battered violin,
enough to cause a woman

warming herself under five skirts
to throw back her head and sing.

Frayed strings. Scorched throat of song.

First it vanishes into thin air,
then the air enters us.

ELEGY WITH MORNING GLORIES

They climb trellis, porch rails, drain spout,
all the way to the roof—a spectacular year,
so passersby stop, and two women argue
over whether or not they're real. Sad thought—

like the time I woke up wondering why
a month has thirty days, until walking home
that night I looked up and saw: Oh, the moon.
How could I forget? Dear City

with your houses packed tight, yellow white white,
your night-black alleys and vacant lots; Unreal
City of shadows, with no moon until
it's high overhead, and then who looks up,

fixed as we are on curbs and sidewalk bricks
upended by roots? Dear City of the stroke
that shook my mother's tree, made her a person
I never met, one who looked at the pool

outside her building and asked what it was—
nineteen years in that place watching her husband
dive, and now it could have been concrete
or the sky he disappeared into and came back out;

City whose crows made her cover her ears
and cry, *stop, stop!*—same voice she used to scold,
only now more shattered, this woman I once
displeased, I, the crow, the crasher, my taste for trash,

always wearing something that raised her brow,
dizzying myself under blurry stars, coming home late,
and talking, talking, which was against the rules
in our house where so much was kept unspoken—

I never thought she'd grow so fragile, so lost
looking out the window, she'd ask if that streetlight
was the moon. If so, think how many we'd have
lining the roads, each one disposable, replaceable.

She who was my start, my star, has burned out,
and though her light still flickers in the blue
dusk she loved, the blue flowers that unswirl
each morning, though I think I see her

in a white sun hat arguing they must be real
or they couldn't climb so high, she is gone,
and nowhere beside any trellis, or any doorsill
in this city, will there ever be another.

BELMULLET

To see where I came from, I'm looking at stones,
at *Johns* and *Marys*, at twenty-eight *Nearys*
in a County Mayo graveyard, each with a pot
of primroses, a plot with white chips of gravel.

If the Irish love talk, my family's silence
seemed to ask, Who wants to go back
to rotten potatoes and patched-up boats,
horse thievery and peat? Who needs long roots

and old wars? Those sealed lips clearly said,
Better to shrug it all off, scrape the sod
from your boots and glad-hand the new world,
let mild winds drift above gravity's grip.

But what wind doesn't come from elsewhere?
Now that those Nearys are nearly gone,
and there's no one to ask whose history
is swelling my knuckles, crimping my face,

I want to be part of a line tethered somewhere,
if only by sea swells, by gusts I love best
when they batter. So I stand among stones
cut deep with my name, not knowing

if the bones rusting here in this ground
are related. But since my family left
no word, I tell these Nearys, if they'll have me,
I'd be pleased to be ghosted by them

in their Wellies and wool, their prayer beads
and pints, their eyes creased by sea glitter
and those minor chords with bent notes
piercing the soul. I'd be pleased

to root myself in this town where tides rise
and sink into sludge, this river mouth littered
with bike frames, clumps of mussels,
and plastic paint buckets—my roots in this junk

the water will nudge and cover again,
as it pours through the inlet, swirling with foam.
Is this where I come from? I kneel down
to finger the gouged letters and half-think,

half-say to this long line of Marys and Johns,
these twenty-eight Nearys: If we all come
to the same end, surely it's not just malarkey
and lark song spiraling up, then plummeting

silently down, surely by sun glint and gull,
by that long ago swallowed sadness,
by sea gut and gravel and wind-wild sky,
these stones that name you name me as well.

AT THE WINDOW

If the doctor's new machine is right, my eyes
are turning into old window glass, warped,
distorted at a thousand points, watching
the moon's fine edge start to fray. But it's spring,

and as if our rooms perched in its branches,
a flowering tree fills the windows. How easy
to say *as if*—as if we were that couple of tiny
Northern Parulas, flitting from limb to limb,

as if we had flown all night, then dropped down
through power lines to feed at first light,
exhausted and starving, intent on the journey,
impelled to breed, breed, always more life.

My grandmother of the Coke-bottle lenses,
of the enormous blue eyes flying close
to the glass like a creature about to crash,
used to recite when she stumbled, "'I see,'

said the blind man when he bumped into the light,"
which I only recalled after slamming into
the plate glass I must have thought was a door—
or didn't think at all, lost inside my head,

as I charged full speed into spectacle-snap,
black-eye smack, at which I saw suddenly
how much I didn't see at all, with a whole
restaurant watching. When a bird flies

into glass does it pass from stun to sob,
and have to make up a new song, or does it
shake off the shock and go on where it was headed
all along, forget reflection? "I once . . . was blind,

but now I see," John Newton wrote, and then
gave up his slave ship to grieve all the ruin
he had wrought. But *how* did he come to see—
what shock, what light shattered the old lens?

_____

154

Until I really looked, I thought geese flew
in those perfect V's we were taught in school,
which would make this flock heading north not
geese at all, with their constantly changing stream

of unraveling threads, their one straggler
wildly flapping to catch up, that outsider
squawking a different tune. Now a small breeze
flies into the tree, so its blossoms flutter,

and a few tear loose to rise, to drift briefly
in the otherwise unseeable air,
that invisible substance we call nothing
and can't live two minutes without.

OUT OF NOWHERE

Slow drum brush, the Hammond B-3
    comping a solo sax, and nothing
        on your mind but the ice in your glass
shifting like notes played one at a time,
    like minutes melting in the dark drift
        of everything past, old goals, scores
wiped clean as the barkeep's tumblers.
    Nobody wants to scratch, to scorch, to fold.
        Yet tonight you think what else is there,
as you flash on the schoolroom sign
    from years ago, telling you "Zero
        is the number of things you have
when you have nothing." Nothing tonight
    but the sax handing off the lead
        to the organ's bluesy prayer,
as you close your eyes, and slow dance
    yourself, empty-handed, letting
        your one heart do nothing but go on.
What else is there? Night turns blue
    and an old fear fills your mind—
        one wrong move, all you could lose.
Another round, and it's all round,
    washed in an amber swirl, where you
        know things you can never say,
though they keep you awake, safe
    from the bluff of pride, that bright lie
        you crashed from years ago
and don't want back. Whatever you lack
    you'll take this ballad's slow drag,
        its low-down mellow sound,
the Hammond's soulful plea pitched
    to the heart's bittersweet beat
        hitting the bottom of this tune,
as the sax stretches out its closing bars,
    wanting nothing more than to linger
        here, where a voice—it could be yours—
rises out of midnight's throat, to give
    this song and everything it knows
        a lone and barely whispered, *Yes.*

ELECTION DAY

Falling on the steps of city hall, the light
this late afternoon infuses the whole sky
and bathes these poor little trees of heaven
stuck in concrete. From all sides, flooding down,

light slants across ruddy brick storefronts,
streaks along cables, glitters up from the bay,
and now, as I turn west toward the hospital,
here's the moon, the Cheshire moon, grinning

bright as a politician's promise, only better,
not favoring a few, but shining for anyone
who stops to gaze at this sky, which not even
the coldest facts can make less marvelous

just now, before the tabulations begin.
And here's the hospital, grinding on, full
of wires and tubes, trays of food, socks that
puff up and down so my friend's legs don't clot.

Isn't it wonderful?—her loopy rainbow grin,
her dozing off mid-sentence, waking surprised,
to say, "Oh, hello," as if I just arrived.
And now when I say good-bye and step out,

the sky's so deep I want to stuff the ballot box,
voting for earth all over again, happy to shiver
in the glow, as the first stars poke through
this impossible to name, not-yet-midnight blue,

letting it pour over me—glorious night,
the brightening moon, below which we turn
in endless space, all of us afloat, held
by invisible strings, though we feel so solid,

so full of our own weight. Lord, let me stand here
feeling nothing but this moment, spinning
and not dizzy, not yet facing the election results.
Let the bass from this passing car pulse through me

as the tattered man leaning on the streetlight
stops another, just to ask the name of his dog,
nothing more, just to say that name, *Herbie,*
and knuckle his ears. Amazing: Two men,

one in a fine suit, one in frayed tweed, stop
and chat, shake hands, each grinning as they part—
here, under this glowing sky, the polls still open,
and the moon above, new, all over again.

PEARS, UNSTOLEN

I was stopped on the sidewalk by pears
glowing on their tree like antique ornaments
with flaking paint, a green metallic shimmer
hinting at yellow, mottled with a few flecks of red.

As light flickered over them, they seemed
to flutter like candles in the leaves.
But no—they were pears, and probably hard,
I told myself, probably inedible, and holding

their juices tight, if they had juices at all.
Besides, something was pitting them like brass,
splotching, as if trying to spoil. Still, I wanted them.
I wanted that September light licking each fruit,

so it seemed lit from without and within,
a fleshy tallow. I wanted the season's clock
stopped before the next strike, stopped in this
amber afternoon, my walk halfway,

the shiny leaves just starting to curl,
but still far from falling, and the pears
half hidden among them like birds singing
so sweetly you step closer, peer in,

careful, careful, wanting to touch that song,
but not squelch it. I stood there wanting
to hoard time, a thief wanting to steal
a song I couldn't hear, a fool believing

there's something sweet that won't disappoint,
that pears in the hand could be anything
like pears dreamed in the mind, or one moment
stopped could keep the rest from rotting.

But what's so bad, a thief will ask: How is
plucking a piece of fruit worse than worms
tunneling in, bees sating themselves
on that honeyed light, or mold blotching it?

Maybe a saint has an answer to that,
something about how too much sweetness spoils,
or how another sweetness grows within.
For weeks I went back and forth, stopping

at the tree, watching first one pear let go
of its limb, then others begin to fall,
flickering briefly like coals in the grass,
before they shrivel, letting their seeds slip out.

"That's the way it goes," mutters the thief.
"As scripture says they must," muses the saint,
while a few last pears glow on their brittle stems
and the wind-strummed boughs bend toward earth.

THE AGING SINGER

Her mouth is cut with crevices
like a marionette's. That little pout,
so flirty in youth, has turned to a scowl.
Still, the voice—it's all sugar and satin, grit,
tough mama strut, then down-on-the-knee
bluesy plea. She can make one word go on
and on—*Oh Lord, puh-leeeze*—rising higher
till we teeter on a ladder top—*send me*—

while the drum nail-guns, the guitar climbs its frets
adding rung after rung, as if to reach heaven
on sound alone. But—*Lord, Lord*—
she's been around, seen how it topples,
so drops to the gutter of her range,
the strain where gospel shifts from style
to soul wrestling its angel, worn and wounded,
but not letting go. *Lord, please send me*—

and in this small venue she must feel us
listening, our separate thoughts silenced,
as she pours herself out, this diva backed
by young men half amused, half awed, a little
bored, and silenced now, by her raised arm,
as she steps out beyond their licks,
hand beating time on her rippling thigh.
Gone, whatever we thought it took

to make a show, just this voice now, all rust
and cut glass—*send me*—gouging her face,
raking that throat, hardly a voice at all, nothing
left but the lowest note she can score—
someone to—she barely mouths the phrase,
head bowed, mic dropped to her side, and us
on the edge of our seats, as the last
unspoken word fills our minds.

Wisconsin Poetry Series

Edited by RONALD WALLACE

(B) = Winner of the Brittingham Prize in Poetry
(FP) = Winner of the Felix Pollak Prize in Poetry
(4L) = Winner of the Four Lakes Prize in Poetry

Places/Everyone (B) • Jim Daniels

Show and Tell • Jim Daniels

Darkroom (B) • Jazzy Danziger

And Her Soul Out of Nothing (B) • Olena Kalytiak Davis

My Favorite Tyrants (B) • Joanne Diaz

Talking to Strangers (B) • Patricia Dobler

The Golden Coin (4L) • Alan Feldman

Immortality (4L) • Alan Feldman

A Sail to Great Island (FP) • Alan Feldman

The Word We Used for It (B) • Max Garland

A Field Guide to the Heavens (B) • Frank X. Gaspar

The Royal Baker's Daughter (FP) • Barbara Goldberg

Gloss • Rebecca Hazelton

Funny (FP) • Jennifer Michael Hecht

The Legend of Light (FP) • Bob Hicok

Sweet Ruin (B) • Tony Hoagland

Partially Excited States (FP) • Charles Hood

Ripe (FP) • Roy Jacobstein

Saving the Young Men of Vienna (B) • David Kirby

Falling Brick Kills Local Man (FP) • Mark Kraushaar

Last Seen (FP) • Jacqueline Jones LaMon

The Lightning That Strikes the Neighbors' House (FP) • Nick Lantz

You, Beast (B) • Nick Lantz

The Explosive Expert's Wife • Shara Lessley

The Unbeliever (B) • Lisa Lewis

Slow Joy (B) • Stephanie Marlis

Acts of Contortion (B) • Anna George Meek

Bardo (B) • Suzanne Paola

Meditations on Rising and Falling (B) • Philip Pardi